MR. MONDAY and OTHER
TALES of JEWISH AMSTERDAM

Five Star Publications, Inc.
Chandler, AZ

MR. MONDAY and OTHER TALES of JEWISH AMSTERDAM

by MEYER SLUYSER

TRANSLATED BY MELS SLUYSER

© Copyright 2005

Five Star Publications, Inc.
P.O. Box 6698
Chandler, AZ 85246-6698
(480) 940-8182
FAX (480) 940-8787
www.MrMonday.com

Library of Congress Cataloging-in-Publication Data

Sluyser, M. (Meyer), 1901-1973.
  Mr. Monday : and other tales of Jewish Amsterdam / Meyer Sluyser.
  p. cm.
1. Jews--Netherlands--Amsterdam--Social life and customs--20th century.
2. Jews--Netherlands--Amsterdam--Anecdotes. 3.   Amsterdam (Netherlands)--Ethnic relations. I. title: Mister Monday. II. Title.
  DS135.N5A655 2004
  949.2'352004924--dc22

                                                                    2004009963

Credits

Marken Alley, Mr. Monday, My Yiddishe Grandma, How Zelig Missed Out on Two Inheritances, and *My Father and Mr. Lebovitz* originally appeared in *Die en die is er nog*, published by F.G. Kroonder in Bussum, The Netherlands, 1956.

Wage Earners, At the Opera, and *Backgrounds* originally appeared in *Er groeit gras in de Weesperstraat*, published by Het Parool/De Vrije Pers, 1958.

The Building, General Eisenhower Called Him The Greatest Living Expert on Security and *Yesterday Never Returns* originally appeared in *Als de dag van gisteren*, published by Het Parool/De Vrije Pers, 1957.

Weekdays and the Sabbath and *Disputes* originally appeared in *Hun lach klinkt van zover*, published by Het Parool/De Vrije Pers, 1959.

Publisher
Linda F. Radke

Project Manager
Susan L. DeFabis

Book Design
Barbara Kordesh
bkordesh@insightbb.com

CONTENTS

MARKEN ALLEY

Every time I walk through Marken Alley nowadays, I am amazed that the few houses that are still there are standing so close together. In my youth the alley where I grew up formed a small gully in the massive block of Amsterdam houses. It was gloomy nearly all day there. Only around three o'clock in the afternoon, when the sun shone on the cobblestones, bright lights and sharp shadows were cast on the pavement, and that occurred only during a few summer weeks.

You can see that there were more houses in those days. They were pulled down later and no new ones were added. Now the alley is like a set of teeth out of which the dentist has pulled a tooth here, a molar there, and over there another tooth, whether it hurt or not. My parents' house is gone too, and maybe that's the reason why it's so difficult for me to recognise the old alley. Somehow I have the feeling that I've dreamed it all, that it is a phantom street.

The houses haven't subsided from old age. People have lent a helping hand. In the icy cold winter of 1944 when the inhabitants of Amsterdam were without fuel, they pulled out the floors of the houses which the Jews had left behind, empty. Later, they stole the beams, the doors, the window frames. And after that, even the joists from the roof.

There was no furniture in the houses then—that had already been taken away by the Nazis. The residents had previously moved, not with furniture vans, but with a simple rucksack on their back and a cap on their head. From Marken Alley they travelled to the East, destination Auschwitz, Mauthausen, Sobibor.

They were born in the slums of Amsterdam, rich people, poor ones, street vendors, shopkeepers, workers. Dark-haired, red-haired, blondes, brunettes. They lived their little lives close to each other in this congested neighbourhood. Each one a small planet in the solar system of his own family, together they formed their universe. But it was written that all should die the same death, somewhere in Eastern Europe. There they crossed the thin line at the end of their journey.

Nobody knows where their bones lie. A few of them are lucky, they have a son—a *kaddish*—or a next of kin who got off alive. The few who have survived from the Holocaust bear a letter and a number tattooed on their left arm, indelibly.

When the shivering people of Amsterdam in the winter of 1944 pulled down the houses of Marken Alley, the memory of the former inhabitants was already fading. The portraits that had once hung on the walls of their living rooms lay scattered between rubbish. Removed from their frames, because wooden frames are excellent fuel for heaters.

The photographs lay there for some time in the rain and the snow. Then the paper became soggy and torn. A gust of wind blew away the shreds. Now, nobody knows anymore what the people looked like before they left.

A handful of Amsterdam Jews have survived judgement day. When they are together, one of them says musing "I don't know why we deserve to still be here."

The other says "We *don't* deserve it."

Nobody laughs. They never say "That one and that one has died."

They always say "That one and that one is still here."

Sometimes they talk about the days when the family was united on this side of the thin wall. It is always in their minds.

With words they try to replace the portraits which have been scattered in the wind. A photograph is really a funny thing, a picture that pretends to be more than it has a right to. It tries to cling onto a second that has disappeared irrevocably into eternity.

Recently, the city-councillors of Amsterdam have decided to pull down the remains of the former Jewish district. Next year the walls of the houses will be torn down. When the debris has been cleared away, they will build a highway right across it.

Those who knew the old district tell me "Write down your memories before it is too late."

I believe I should. Our memory is like a sand beach, the footsteps of the people who lived here are printed in the sand, but soon high tide will wipe them out. What will be left of the old neighbourhood in ten or twenty years time? Already grass is growing in the streets between the cobblestones. Soon the old generation will have carried its sadness into the grave.

Superstitious folks say that a house has a soul. I know this to be true. The house is built as a cold, lifeless object out of bricks and mortar. But people marry and are happy within its walls—a piece of their happiness remains in the house. A child is born—another thread of happiness is added. Someone dies and a bedroom suddenly becomes a holy place. Then the house has a soul. In those derelict ruins that remain of the old Jewish neighbourhood, a thousand threads together form the remembrance of its past.

"Write down your memories before you forget…"

I wander along the alley, between the houses, aimlessly. Spirits speak to me, but I cannot hear their voices.

I walk like a *Golem*.

I cross the threshold between being and non-being. Days become hours, and hours seconds.

I am lying again in the warm bed on the third floor of our house in Marken Alley. When I close my eyes, I see on the inside of my eyelids the neighbourhood as I knew it during the forty years before the Great Sorrow.

The streets, the houses, the little front-rooms and back-rooms. A thousand cubes, a bewildering honeycomb.

In all these cubby-holes people live. The walls are too narrow to constrain their exuberant bustle. It bursts out through the open doors. It presses through the open windows. It spills through the streets. The living river eddies between the high banks of the houses. Pushcarts with their trade stick out like islands in the stream.

People, people, people.

I know all their faces. Names drift on the slow waves of memory. Every face is a novel, each life is different.

As long as I keep my eyes closed the neighbourhood is still there. The houses have not fallen in decay, the people live. I see this image very sharply, as though I hold an aerial photo in my hand.

It is not true that Time is a flowing stream. Time stands still, and we travel along it from memory to memory.

Past and Present lie along the same line.

Yesterday and Today are parts of the same reality.

MR. MONDAY

OUR NEIGHBOURHOOD COBBLERS NAME was Monday. Mr. Monday we all called him. That was not his real name, but no one ever called him anything else. His real name sounded somewhat like Mozejekofsky or Moskofsky or Moshekofsky or something equally unpronounceable.

Mr. Monday was not what you'd call a real Dutchman, either. His father and mother came to Holland from Poland or Russia when he was about six years old, because a bloody pogrom was raging in their home country. Originally it had been the intention of the family to move on to America, but there were many such Jews as themselves in Amsterdam, so they decided to stay there.

The family rented a back room on the third floor of a house in Manege Street in the Jewish quarter. Because Dutch people sprained their tongues on their outlandish name, they took unto themselves the name of "Maandag" (Monday)... just to make it easy.

Why Monday and not Tuesday or Wednesday? Perhaps because they wanted an easy sounding name starting with the letter "M" like in their real name, and that it just happened to be a Monday that day.

When they had lived there for a couple of years, they rented the front room too. With it they got a kitchen and a small storeroom. It seemed a palace to them

Their son, *our* Mr. Monday, became the personal apprentice to a master cobbler. After he got married he rented the basement of the house to live in and to start a shoemaking shop himself. The back room of the basement became the sitting room of the young couple's home. A shed attached to the back entrance completed their residence.

For years on end our cobbler lived and worked in that draughty and wet basement. If anyone ever asked him why he didn't look for a better place, he used to reply, "If the good G-d Himself lived in Manege Street, people would still ask, 'Why don't you move?'"

Furthermore, he was very attached to Manege Street. As a matter of fact, most of the immigrants from Eastern Europe showed a definite preference for living in or around that street because close to it, around the corner in Church Street, they had their own synagogue.

During the service, that little "shul" resounded with a passionate religious zeal. Those praying Russians beat themselves on the breast in a frenzy of atonement and submission. The melodies of their ancient incantations were full of wild-sounding tones. The Dutch Jews who attended their services felt as though they were hearing and seeing things that they remembered without really knowing from where. These sounds seemed to come from centuries ago, when their own great-grandfathers, with long curly locks for sideburns, walked around wearing black *kaftans* down to their ankles, and hats trimmed with fox fur.

But let me not forget our cobbler, Mr. Monday!

His name was a rich source for an endless line of jokes.

The most common was, when he made his rounds from door to door asking if there was work for him to be done.

"Good morning, Mrs. Cohen, got some work for the cobbler? Any shoes or straps need fixing?" he would say.

"Well, good morning to you too, Mr. Monday. But whatever made you come today? Today isn't your day, you should know that. You should have come yesterday. Today is Tuesday, not Monday."

To that kind of remark Mr. Monday responded with a little smile. Painless jokes he could appreciate as much as the next person.

Besides repairing shoes, he also sold lottery tickets on the side. In his shop window he had a sign showing when the lottery prizes would be drawn. I remember one day when he tried to sell a ticket to us and my father said very seriously, "I won't play in the lottery this time. I don't trust it. You know other times I always buy a ticket from you, but not this time. I've discovered that it's just a great big swindle. They're not honest, those people who are in charge of the lottery."

"How can you say such a thing...?" said Mr. Monday, protesting. "The government..." Then he hesitated, because, to be truthful, he did not know what Father was aiming at.

Father replied with a reproachful look, "I tell you quite frankly, I don't trust those lottery people of yours. They are swindlers."

"What? You don't trust them? But everything is honest through and through. It's a national lottery, it is the government...the government!"

"Yes I know that, but still I don't trust them. Right

now, at this very moment they already know who is going to draw the big jackpot number. In fact, they already know the man's name."

Now, Mr. Monday was sure that my Father was out of his mind. However, it was characteristic of him never to show that he was angry with a customer. He did not flatter customers, but he did not argue with them, either. Speaking very calmly, he tried to explain to my father that the State lottery is not an ordinary lottery but that it is run by the Government. Children from an orphanage draw the tickets from a big drum, and everything is carried out in a fair and honest way.

"So why do you believe that the name of the person who will win the big prize is already known?"

"I have read it!" said my father.

"Read it. Where have you read it?", cried Mr. Monday desperately.

"In your shop, in your own shop. You and nobody else will get the big money prize. You have a poster in your shop window saying *"First prize in the State Lottery Monday!"*

Our cobbler could take that as a joke, too. At least, he appeared to like it because he repeated the story to all his customers.

Nevertheless, he was not a funny man himself, in fact he was rather mournful. Around his mouth lay the mild, somewhat sorrowful lines of the philosopher who has seen the world and has forgiven it for its wrongs. For instance, if anybody ever reported to him that a certain mutual acquaintance had behaved in a particularly base way, Mr. Monday used to remark, "Nebbish, nobody could be so low just for the fun of it."

That kind of forgiveness was seldom understood, and certainly not appreciated. Especially when it was clear that the individual in question had committed his foul deed, not because he had been forced to, but only because he derived pleasure and satisfaction from it.

When that fact was pointed out to our cobbler, he would comment "If that man is such a *chazzer* (a pig) just for fun, you should pity him twice. Nebbish, nebbish."

Over most of the jokes he told, lay a veil of mournful compassion. He laughed because he did not want to cry. One story that he called his pet joke went like this:

"There was a Polish Jew and he said, 'I am proud to be a Jew, because if I weren't proud of it, I would still be a Jew. So I might as well be proud of it.'"

Problems that excited others, merely moved Mr. Monday to remark, "People, human beings. What more can you expect from them than that they are what they are. And that doesn't amount to much.

Or: "What's all the excitement about? In a hundred years from now, we'll all be dead and gone."

Or: "It is only when you are in need of friends that you discover that you are alone in the world."

Perhaps he inherited his philosophical attitude from the sages of old among our people. He let slip out easily that he was a distant relative of the Ba'al Shem, the Keeper of the Name, the legendary Jewish sage who was worshipped as a prophet in Eastern Europe. At the small Russian shul in Church Street, everyone was aware of this supposed family connection. When Mr. Monday entered the synagogue, an almost silent whispering ran through the gathering of praying men because after all, he was small ray of the great light.

If you saw Mr. Monday sitting in the front room of his basement shop, you wouldn't suspect what a really strange person he was. His head was always covered with a dark cap, the symbol of his religion. On the table in front of him stood an oil lamp that burned all day. Between him and that light was a large glass bowl filled with water. An object like that was called an ordinal and it served as a lens and light amplifier.

He had quite a number of customers and from his earnings he could have lived quite comfortably if he had been an ordinary man. In reality he was a barrel full of contradictions and inner doubts, a restless seeker and at the same time a musing dreamer. The complexity of his psyche you would begin to suspect only when, in his dark basement room against the wall you inspected his two small cupboards filled with books. One cupboard contained Judaica. Some prayer books and commentaries written by pious men were very rare. In particular, one dusty book filled Mr. Monday with uncommon pride, so rare was that volume.

"I would rather lose an arm than lose that book," he confided to me. "Even in the famous Straschun Library in Vilno, no copy of that volume is to be found."

The other cupboard contained books about the physical sciences but the titles seemed to have been picked by a medieval alchemist. Only centuries-old books were arranged on those warped shelves. *The Laws of Nature* by the Abbé Nolet and *About the Behaviour of Mercury in the Full Moon* or *The Magnet Stone and the Scorpion, a Treatise on Machines that do not Require an External Moving Power.*

Since there were no books of more recent date, Mr. Monday's interest in natural science was rather out of date,

as you may have guessed. As a scholar, he lived at least three
hundred years too late. The object of his study wasn't
exactly modern either, he was trying to build a machine
that was driven by perpetual motion. In the little shed at
his back door lay the remnants and wreckage of oddly
contrived instruments. On the shelves stood jam pots, grey
with dust filled with mysterious powders and solutions. An
alchemist's workshop. That rubbish was from the time Mr.
Monday thought that he could find the unfindable by
empirical means, by trying out many things and hoping for
results. He was only cured of that belief after he nearly
caused the whole of Manege Street to go up in smoke.
After that explosion, he did not follow the empirical way
anymore but chose to seek the *perpetuum mobile* in a theo-
retical way only. He shared his nightly hours equally
between Talmud and the Abbé Nollet. "First you must
study, practice must wait," he explained his new approach.

Modern people would have become prey to restlessness
with such a split of their psyche, but Mr. Monday did not
know what a nervous ulcer was. Somewhere he had found
the synthesis of his two bookcases. He remained serene,
nothing could destroy the rest of his soul, neither endless
study nor domestic troubles. And domestic troubles he had,
really more than one man could bear. In his family life all
adversities seemed to be aimed mercilessly at him. He had
a son called Elkan whose birth had been a fight against
death and his mother had never recovered full health again.
Mrs. Monday became partially paralysed, and she complained of water that made her legs swell like overstuffed
sausages.

Elkan himself was an imbecile. Mostly he sat in the
corner of the workshop, saliva dripping from his mouth.

He could scarcely talk. When he was thirteen years old, he behaved like a toddler of three.

Medicines for his sick wife and imbecile son cost Mr. Monday a lot of money and in order to get a little extra income he started a new profession—on the side, you must understand. He made up poems to order. People came to him in the evening after the shop was closed and gave him orders to write poems to be recited at wedding parties and other special occasions. They ladled out information about the bride and bridegroom and how their engagement was arranged and more of those kinds of details. Then Mr. Monday put it all into rhyme and rhythm.

Sometimes his customers would ask him to insert political hints in those doggerels, for example a sly word or two, that the bridegroom lent his ear to political orations instead of attending synagogue and listening to the rabbi. Mr. Monday never objected to putting them in. He considered himself responsible only for the form of the poems, nobody could blame him for the contents and subtle hints. By setting that rule for himself, he eliminated the possibility of any conflict of conscience in his own political being, because he himself had certain strong views on politics. He was a socialist, but of a strange sort, he was a supporter of the Polish Bund, a political organisation of the Polish ghetto ideologically close to Marxism. Mr. Monday sympathised with the faction of the Bund which was opposed to Zionism. Every week he received a small periodical, Yiddish text in Hebrew letters, the organ of the Bund. The paper came from Lodz, in Poland.

Although he had lived in Holland for so long, our cobbler's political attention was drawn tightly to the problems of the Bund. About those problems he talked with his neighbours in Manege Street. He argued that the Jews in Poland should be recognised as an official minority with full rights and full duties. Yes, sir, duties, too! The Bund wanted to make Poland a socialist fatherland for the Polish Jews as well as for anyone else.

Mr. Monday explained those political ideas to me many a time. I could not argue with him because once he straddled his hobbyhorse, one could scarcely get a word in edgewise. Then round about 1930 a book was published that was written by the French journalist Albert Londres, who had made a swing around Eastern Europe and described the situation of the Jews there.

I had read that book and told Mr. Monday something about it. Later, when a Dutch translation was published, I brought a copy to our cobbler.

He read it with a critical eye, although he had never set a foot on Polish soil after he was six years of age. But so close was his spiritual contact that with expert knowledge he exposed the articles to his judgement. His final opinion of the book was a profound evaluation.

"This man plainly has a heart, but he cannot creep into the brains of a Polish Jew," he told me. "He saw everything and does not suppress a single fact in telling it. Yet he understood nothing of what he has observed. You should go there yourself Meyer, and check up, then you will see that I am right."

So I have to thank our shoemaker for the idea of a journalistic journey through Eastern Europe in 1932. Mr. Monday gave me introductions to people he had never met and whom he knew only from the weekly Bund newspaper. He put a scrap of paper into my hand on which he had written in Hebrew characters the name of a very rare book.

"If you should get to Vilno, ask in the Straschun Library whether they have a copy of it," he instructed me, handing me a title slip.

When I was in Vilno I went to the Straschun Library right away. In a back street, leaning against the wall of the old synagogue, I found two small rooms, shacks really. There, in an old bookcase, were kept the hand writings of Gaon, the famous sage—handwritings for which famous collectors offered to pay a king's ransom.

But Vilno was the Town of the Book, and the Jews are the People of the Book. They did not sell their ancient manuscripts.

Dr.Rubinstein, the librarian, looked carefully at the scrap of paper that Mr. Monday had given to me.

"Do you have that book?" I asked.

"No, I am sorry, but no. But you come from Holland, don't you? There is a copy in Amsterdam, owned by a certain Mosejekofsky of Moskosofsky or Moshekofsky or something. In short, this Mr.Rubinstein knew that Mr. Monday possessed the book. It was the rare book Mr. Monday had shown me in his cupboard of Judaica. That shoemaker of ours, sometimes he could be a vain man!

From Poland I wandered to Pods in Karpatho Russia. The area had been Russian, then Czech, and is, I believe, Russian again today. I travelled through Rumania too, back through Bukovina and northward, with a detour via Munkacevo, to Pods once more.

There I began to know a world whose existence I had only vaguely suspected. It was not a pleasant world. Poverty, exploitation, prejudice, bigotry and backwardness were the parapets against which the Zionists stormed. Palestine was more than just an idea, more than the centuries-old yearning for the land with which the Jews were tied by mystical bonds. It was the New Era that strove to triumph.

Up to that day I had thought that Mr. Monday represented a rare human specimen, an eccentric being, a unique case. But Eastern Europe fairly teemed with people like him. They lived spiritually in the Middle Ages. Surrounded by black misery, they were dreamers and seekers, thinkers and sages.

Dualistic characters, they were. Mildly contemptuous of earthly troubles, yet at the same time gripped by the strong desire to get more from the social cake than their neighbour. Men of the Book, and at the same time small business men who wanted to make money by any means or schemes they could devise.

In Mukacevo in the Micaciemikagassa, I visited the miracle-rabbi Spira. When I mentioned the subject of Zionism to the rabbi, he exploded into a revealing diatribe against his archenemies, the Zionists. "Those Zionists…Communists they are, all of them!" Spira raged. "I have cursed them and I will curse them again. They undermine everything we have built here. They have even got the Town Council so meshuggah that it named two streets after their leaders. Now we have here the Bialik Street and the Yehuda Halevi Street. That Bialik, he is a swindler and a brigand, and he eats pork, too. And that

Yehuda Halevy, that is not the famous one of a thousand
. years ago. No, that is a brother-in-law of Bialik, and he runs
a shop in ham and lard in Bialystock!"

When, after returning to Holland, I had written about
my observations, Mr. Monday reproved me, telling me that
I had observed Eastern Europe with the eyes of a man from
the West. Hadn't I seen that within the boundaries of the
ghetto, romanticism and art flowered bountifully? I had
disappointed him because I hadn't seen that the Jews of
Eastern Europe found warmth in their own surroundings.
That there they were secure against new, undesirable influ-
ences. It was not all so hopelessly black on black, as I had
described it, he pointed out to me.

The articles that resulted from the trip were published
in the newspaper I was working for and later appeared in
book form. One night I walked over to Manege Street to
present Mr. Monday with a copy of the book. After all, it
was partly his brainchild, wasn't it? He looked at the cover,
read the title and said pensively, "You have chosen the
wrong title. *Jews in Distress*? No, that is not the right title."

He thought for a moment and then said slowly, "It
should have been *'Here you can read how the ghetto has
wronged the Jews.'*"

Years pass by. It is May 10, 1940. The Nazis invade Holland.

When the blond gorillas came to fetch Mr. Monday and
his imbecile son and his sick wife, our cobbler put his
resistance plan in operation. He barricaded the entrance to
his basement. The dusty jam pots with their mysterious
contents were taken from the shed. He had bought bleaching powder, buckets full of bleaching powder. And many

bottles of hydrochloric acid. When the anti-Semites came, he would pour acid on the bleaching powder. No enemy would be able to pass. He knew. He had studied science and the mysteries of the old alchemists. He would fight as a modern Maccabee. That was the synthesis of Talmud and Abbé Nollet.

The gorillas just kicked the buckets onto the pavement. They never even suspected that they escaped poisoning by chlorine gas. Then they dragged the family into the street. Mr. Monday resisted. They put a pistol against his neck…A shot. He died instantly.

"Hear, O Israel…"

And what happened to the hundreds of thousands like him who had remained in Bedzyn, Lodz, Lwow, Crakow, and Warsaw?

People all over the world know the epic story of the revolt in the Warsaw ghetto. A modern army against a hundred and fifty thousand defenseless people. Tanks against sticks and knives. Machine guns against the tools of garment workers and cobblers. Much had the ghetto wronged the Jews, but it had not been able to break their courage. In the end, in their finest hour they fought like lions, with nails and claws. The revolt lasted long. Men, women, young and old people fought till their last breath. Nobody hoped. Nobody asked for grace. Maccabee had arisen and Bar Kochba, and they fought the good, the holy fight, as did Mr. Monday, when his turn came in Manege Street in the Jewish quarter of Amsterdam.

"Hear, O Israel…"

∞

WAGE EARNERS

ONE LATE AFTERNOON I had an appointment with a tailor at his workshop, number so-and-so on the New Achtergracht in Amsterdam. He explained to me how to get there.

"After you have passed through the front door, you have to go through a long corridor and then you climb an iron staircase. Then you go through another corridor and at the end of it is the door to my workshop. You can't miss it."

But I did miss it, because once in the first long corridor I got completely rattled. The smell in that old factory drove away all sense of the present. I heard myself say aloud: "Good Lord, this is father's old factory!"

After so many long years, the sensuous sweet odour of machine oil, driving belts and sweat still hung within its walls. Smells arouse powerful associations. They intoxicate. They invoke visions…

"What does your father do?"
"He works in the docks."
"*My* father works in the trade…"

Children like to brag about their parents. The "Trade", a word that embraces all the professions of the extensive diamond industry. Twenty thousand diamond workers in a city of little more than half a million souls. Not including the related professions such as the manufacturers of tools, the shops that sell workman's blouses, and the middle class that earns a living from and through the "Trade". For the diamond workers the verb "to work" only has one meaning— "Work" you can only do in the diamond trade. In other professions you toil, slave, grind, drudge.

I will give you an example. One day an unemployed diamond worker is taking a stroll along the quay and he sees another unemployed colleague, dead-beat from toil, climb up out of the hold of a ship with a 50 kilo bale of sugar on his back.

He asks "Aren't you working?"

The children of diamond workers receive instructions in a playful manner. The diamond cutter cannot cut a pear for them without making a brilliant out of it. First he tells the child to remove a very thin slice. "Be careful," he warns. "When the stone loses too much in the cutting, the boss can hang himself."

The pear now has a beautifully smooth and pure form.

"So…and now you make the little table."

The pear diamond gets a smooth upper surface.

"And now the bezels, and here, those are the pavilions. So, now the stone is in the girdle. Making the brilliant you must also learn. See, and now here you…Ai, you've cut too much off. You should have left a culet, now you've botched the stone!"

Bezels, pavilions, culets…For the layman they are all only sides and edges of the diamond. He cannot tell one from the other, but the children recognise them immediately. To muff a stone means that one or more of the sixty-four surfaces does not have exactly the correct size so that it does not let the light fall through the diamond flawlessly. To botch a stone is the worst crime a person can commit.

"Father, may I try again? We can cut off half of the pear and make the stone a bit smaller."

"Smaller? Then you should hear the boss! More than half is lost because you have been muddling!"

The children use expressions of the trade in a metaphorical way. A girl comes home and tells her parents "The teacher has put that little Moppes boy next to me in class so I can help him along. He isn't out of the girdle yet."

That means that the little Moppes boy is a bit backward, because a stone which isn't out of its girdle yet is only half finished.

Although they are all diamond workers, there are significant distinctions in rank and prestige between the various categories. The cleavers form a small select group, they earn more money than the others and therefore feel themselves miles high above the riffraff. The others are jealous and they jeer "You cleavers do not really form the élite, only the Isra-élite!"

The factories are inhabited mostly by polishers and setters. The polishers put the heavy tongs with the lead shell in which the diamond is forged on the swiftly turning disk. They complain, "That setter of ours is a *behayme*. (Behayme is the singular of *behomoth* which means cattle).

The animosity between the two groups stems from the fact that the setter can, in a way of speaking, make or break the earnings of a polisher. Each setter serves five or six polishers. Every time one of the sixty-four tiny planes is exactly in its right place, he gets back the lead shell and on his gas flame he melts the solder. Then he turns the stone slightly in such a way that the next plane can be polished. The polishers sit with their backs to the light of the windows, the setters stand with their backs towards them. The long row of the backs of the polishers forms one side of an alley, the row of backs of the adjusters the other side.

Because they sit back-to-back the polishers jeering call the setters their fart catchers. "Have you heard," they joke to each other, "that they have been asked to take part in the opening of Parliament next September? You didn't know? Well, when the queen comes driving up in her gold coach, our setters will be part of the ceremonial procession, their job is to march right behind the horses to catch the farts."

The children often visit the factory. At noon mother says, "When you have finished eating, you have to run over to the factory. I have a nice pan of baked potatoes for you to take to your father." The potatoes are warmed up on an adjustable light. The potato dishes may also contain stewed cow stomach, onion, meat or boiled fish, and then the factory reeks of the messages of love. But in the titillating smell of food, criminal instincts grow like cucumbers during a thunderstorm. If the owner of the hash lets his attention slacken for an instant, someone else is sure to steal a mouthful from his pan. Then when he complains they reply "What does it matter, one mouthful? You have a pan-full."

One adjuster has a pan with thick soup standing on his heater when he is called to the office of the boss. But he is a man of brains, so he puts a note next to his dish "Don't eat this. I've spit in it."

When he comes back they've written on the paper "We too."

However, unity is restored between polishers and setters when they have sing-songs together. Diamond workers are very fond of music; they seldom miss a performance at the opera and they know all the arias by heart.

At the sing-song in the factory, when the whole repertory of Italians is exhausted, it is the turn of the polishers' songs. One man sings a stanza solo; the chorus strikes up together. Neither the composer of the music nor the writer of the libretto, which was probably originally conceived for a café concert, would recognise their own work, because in the factory, words and music acquire a new atmosphere.

The apprentices are seated at the other side of the polishing mill. They learn the trade well and thoroughly. Sometimes the polishers use them as errand boys for some trifle. The apprentices retaliate by purposely making mistakes. For instance, when the boy is sent out to buy ginger buns, and his boss says "Here is twenty cents. Ten cents for my bun and ten cents for yours". The boy returns later, munching and swallowing, and explains "they only had one bun left, so here's your ten cents back."

Or when an opera will be performed by a famous company from Italy and a monstrously fat polisher tells his apprentice "You go to Carré and book me two seats."

"Two? Is your wife coming with you? I thought she was ill in bed."

"No, I'm going by myself. But tonight I want to sit comfortably and spread myself."

That evening, when the polisher arrives at the opera house, he finds that the two seats the boy has reserved are one behind the other...

Such impudent behaviour is appreciated by the polishers because they too have a fine sense of humour. They poke fun at each other continuously, so how can they be angry when someone kids them in return?

Perhaps they are tolerant towards the young fellows because they recognise themselves as they were once, long ago when they had no children who had to go to school and no wife who needed money for housekeeping. The apprentice is taught the trade like a fish learns to swim. After a few years he cannot live on dry land. That's why all the diamond workers return to the trade sooner or later, even though they've been out of work for a year. They say, "It's a rotten profession, but only when you don't love it you hate it."

The salesmen who hawk their wares in the diamond factories are also a favourite butt of jokes. However, sometimes they manage snide remarks back too. Just listen to this story.

"Have you heard about Levie?"

"Which Levie do you mean?"

"The one who goes with his suitcase along the factories."

"Oh, you mean that Levie. No, what's the matter with him?"

"Last week he was paying a visit to the factory of Boas and he says to a polishers 'You want to buy something of me?' Says the polisher 'No, I don't need anything'."

Says Levie "You don't need shoe-laces?"

"No," says the polisher.

Says Levie, "Then take a carton with pins and needles home to your wife."

Says the polisher "My Sarah has stocked the house full of pins and needles."

Well, Levie keeps going on and on "don't you need this, don't you need that", so finally the polisher says "I have a terrible diarrhoea, don't you have something for that?"

Says Levie "No, not directly. But I do have a necktie for sale with a beautifully matching colour."

The emperor Napoleon, after he had conquered Holland, introduced civil registration for all Dutchmen. This included the Jews. But Jews were known as sons of their fathers. Moses, son of Isaac, was called "Moses ben Yitzchak". This could go on and on, for instance "Avrom ben Shimme ben Ari ben Nehemin". Jewish names were too complicated for the gentlemen at the Town Hall who had been ordered by Napoleon to register them, so they simplified them.

"Who are you?" they ask.

"Schmul, the fishcleaner."

"Good, from now on your name is Samuel "Visschoonmaker" (fishcleaner). That is how bizarre names came into being based on the profession of these people.

"Visschraper" (Fishscraper), "Kuit" (Spawn), "Uienkruier" (Onionbarrowman), "Augurkiesman" (Gherkinman), "Aardewerk" (Crockery), "Porcelein" (Porcelain).

In the long row of people who registered there was a considerable number of clowns.

"And what are you?"

"Seldom at home."

So the clerk wrote down the name he had to carry the rest of his life: "Zeldenthuis" (seldom at home).

"And who are you?"

"Me? I am the good…"

The clerk wrote down "De Goeie" (The Good).

They thought they were fooling that stupid looking civil servant, but in point of fact they really burdened themselves and their descendants right up to the seventy-seventh generation with impossibly sounding names. But look it up, the name "Voddeman" (Rag dealer) was not included, nor "Beneman" (Bone man), so we can conclude that in Napoleon's time business was so bad that even a rag-and-bone dealer could not make a living.

Anyway, rag-and-bone dealer is not really a profession. No boy would ever tell his dad and mum "When I am grown up, I will become a rag-and-bone man." This is because rag-and-bone dealers are made, not born. When there is no work available in the normal professions, the unemployed look for earnings elsewhere. In wintertime they clear away the snow and in summertime they push a cart and sell wares. In no other profession is there so much unemployment as in the diamond trade, so most of the incidental rag-and-bone dealers are really diamond workers.

From the shining stones to the rags and bones...

The rag-and-bone dealers have their own melody. "Voddeeeee" (raaaaags!).

Then a thirty seconds pause.

"Voddeeeee!!!"

They never shout "bones". That is because bones do not yield profit any more since the glue factories have switched to producing artificial glue.

Moreover, you can smell the bones a mile away and they attract a cavalcade of flies which accompany the cart from one street to another. That drives away the customers.

"Voddeeeee!!!" When he chances to meet one of his companions in adversity on the street, the rags dealer says "In seven weeks I have not earned one cent. But perhaps today's my lucky day."

To them the rag trade may be a means of earning their bread, but they have to be satisfied with dry bread, there is no meat on it.

The simple folks in those days dreamed of being able to afford eating meat sandwiches in a sandwich shop. For them that was the crowning luxury. There were many such shops in Amsterdam at the time. In the sandwich shop a beefy man in a white coat cuts lean salted meat into thin slices. Then he places the slices in a freshly cut roll but leaves the meat hanging from the sides like lavish curtains. That is what's called a "normal" roll.

A variation is the "half-and-half" roll, a mixed marriage between boiled liver and meat, joined in holy matrimony by the bread. The precarious wedlock is made spicy by a blob of mustard. Sandwich shop Zuidema in Warmoestreet is famous for another speciality called *The Zuidema Roll* , a misalliance between salt meat and coarse sausage.

In this way, every shop has its gastronomic speciality. *Cohen's* in Damstreet possesses a secret recipe for baked haddock roe. All year Mr.Cohen sells rolls with meat in all forms and concoctions, but when autumn comes, the neat little shop starts to reek of baked haddock roe. The secret of his recipe lies mainly in the smallness of his roes. Says Mr.Cohen proudly "The smaller the roe, the finer the fish."

First he cooks the small morsels until they are just done. He lets them cool down and then fries them in butter. They are eaten piping hot right out of the frying pan between a roll of bread.

One day a man sits in Cohen's shop and orders "Give me another roe sandwich."

He eats five sandwiches, one after another, or maybe ten or a hundred—one can't keep count without a double bookkeeping. The man is in an abyss of roe, with no bottom in sight. He loosens his waistcoat.

"Give me another roe sandwich."

He opens the top buttons of his trousers.

"Give me another roe sandwich."

He has now reached euphoria and starts to belch.

Says Mr.Cohen indignantly, "Mister, you wouldn't do a thing like that in the American Hotel restaurant, would you?" (The American Hotel restaurant is a chic luxury place on Leyden Square).

The man answers between two belches, "To tell you the truth, I did do it in the American Hotel restaurant, and do you know what they told me? "For such bad eating behaviour you should go to Cohen's in Damstreet!"

Insiders know where they can get specialities. At *De Haas* the warm calf meat sandwiches taste best when they have been dipped in fat gravy.

Says a customer " Miss Abrams, will you please dip my calf meat sandwich not once but twice in the gravy?"

Says the waitress sarcastically "What are you—a Jew or an Anabaptist?"

The old-fashioned sandwich shops have disappeared in Amsterdam along with the customers. Although nowadays there are still some sandwich shops they've been reduced from individual institutions to places where they sell anything ranging from Hamburgers to French fries. Ways of earning a living have changed, also. Today, who knows what a real old-fashioned "tout" used to be? That was a strange and fascinating profession, closely connected to the interest of Jews for clothes…

The women seldom buy their clothes in a shop. They do a little dress making themselves, but usually they are customers of some cheap scamstress who lives nearby.

By contrast, the clothes for boys and men are bought in shops, but not directly. Between shopkeeper and customer the tout has claimed his place. Touts invariably are small men, perhaps because the shopkeeper is aware that his customers do not want to feel overwhelmed by their formidable dimensions. The tout has to make the customers believe he has their best interest at heart, to engender trust. So he acts in a subtle manner. His working place is the sidewalk in front of the tailor shop. There are no female touts, not even as an exception. This is because the tout's main function is to address potential customers, and that is what no respectable lady would do. He has to induce them to stand still before the shop-window.

"Are you sure you don't need anything?" he says, addressing a passerby. "It really does not matter if you look, just looking will not cost you a cent. Who knows, maybe there's something here for you, or for someone in your family. Or for a friend."

The person halts in front of the shop, not knowing that he's already lost half of the battle. The tout speaks with a tongue of velvet. He may never become rude, because chutzpah makes people stubborn.

There are touts who can sell someone a set of false dentures at the beginning of the street, and are capable of buying it back at the end of the street at half price. However, such tempters are avoided like the plague. People then would rather make a detour than pass that shop again, because those touts are like tigers lying in ambush. Because touts mainly work on commission, an arrogant one is a bad wage earner. The good tout must be able to pull a face dripping of good fellowship. When he is nice to young children, the mothers must have the proud feeling that he isn't pretending.

"Och, what a schatsie (little darling)," he will say, patting the little girl on the head. "Would you believe it, every day thousands of children pass this way, but such a beauty? No, you see that only once in your life."

The most famous tout of Amsterdam is Joseph Italiaander. In Damstreet he sorts out the passers-by with a roving eye and keen understanding. The first group consists of customers, the second of worthless people. The customers he divided again into groups, first the easy ones whose money burns a hole in their pockets. Secondly, the troublesome ones with whom you have to argue endlessly in order to convince them that they have come to buy. And finally, the bargain hunters who would preferably buy at least a dozen suits for one guilder, with a posh overcoat added as a free extra.

Joseph is an active Union member and there his profession is listed as "accoster". He is also an eloquent supporter of his political party where he is known to talk too much. He does not miss one meeting of that party and when there is an opportunity to ask questions—and there are many of such opportunities—the chairman puts the name Italiaander down automatically as number one on the list of speakers.

Joseph stands up and asks "Mister Chairman, why do I always have to speak first? And then, just when I'm getting into my stride you always interrupt to tell me that I have to make it short because there are so many speakers after me on the list."

Says the Chairman "Exactly, that's why I always put you as number one."

"Can't you put me last just this once?"

"No, because in that case we'll have to hold an extra meeting just for you."

Joseph has not developed this interest in public welfare out of egoistic motives but from a sense of social responsibility. From where he stands in front of his shop near the corner of Damstreet, he has a full view of the Royal Palace on Dam Square. One hundred years ago a mayor lived there and when he died they put on his tombstone "When common people call upon you, care for them like for yourself." That might also be the epitaph of Joseph Italiaander. He roves around busily and quickly on political battlefields. The loquacious little man may seem to many at meetings a troublesome gadfly, but he means well.

Someone stands still before his shop window and Joseph positions himself next to the man. In his high, squeaky voice he says to him "I believe I know you. Aren't you a friend of Maupie Wegloop ("walk away", another odd surname from the time of Napoleon).

There really is a Maupie Wegloop, and it is also true that this person is an acquaintance of Joseph Italiaander. But all the rest is made up. That's the art of accosting. With his eyes closed and his rifle at the wrong shoulder, Italiaander has fired a wild shot. But that experienced tout has put his question with the mysterious timbre in his voice to which few people are impervious. The future customer considers. He really does not know this Maupie Wegloop at all, but why should he disappoint that friendly little man with the happy moon-face smile.

So he answers "Maupie Wegloop…? Yes, indeed I know him." When the man has told this little white lie he is irretrievably lost. Before the spider will let him escape from the web, the little fly has bought a costume or an overcoat, or at least a pair of trousers, or at the very least a silk neckerchief.

But this "mutual acquaintance" ploy does not always work. It can also go like this.

"How are you, sir, beautiful display, don't you think?
I believe I know you, aren't you a certain Zadoks?"

"Indeed, my name is Zadoks. So what?"

"I've heard a lot about you, Mr. Zadoks," Joseph says.

Later he tells at home "Oy, just when I'm saying I've
heard a lot about you, this fellow turns red. Sour he looks,
sour! With two hands you wouldn't be able to describe
how sour that man looks. He snarls at me 'So, you have
heard talk about me, you say? Well, they'll have to prove it
first. I'm good for any amount of money, you remember
that!'

Oy, how was I to know that this fellow has gone bank-
rupt and that they don't trust his bookkeeping. It was in
the newspapers but I hadn't read about it. I couldn't earn
a cent from him."

A good tout has his own secret intelligence service. When
there will be a Bar Mitzvah soon, the news will be brought
to him. The thirteen year-old boy, who will have to recite a
chapter from the Book in Hebrew before the whole congregation in the synagogue, will have to sweat at that
solemn occasion in a traditional costume. It is an old man's
costume. On his head, which of course has to be covered,
he wears a round hat, the Bar Mitzvah hat. For reasons
unknown, that hat is usually bought before the costume
is purchased.

The shop assistant of *The Flying Pot* in the Rapenburg
district is hand in glove with the tout telling him, "Listen,
the Venetiaander family have been here with their little son
to buy the Bar Mitzvah hat."

"Good, thank you for telling me. If I sell them any-thing, one guilder is for you."

So that when a few days later the Venetiaander family, father, mother and the little Bar Mitzvah boy appear on Damstreet, Italiaander jumps to attention. But pa and ma Venetiaander are not that crazy either. They come saunter-ing along, seemingly indifferent. If his spies hadn't informed him, the tout would never suspect that they have come to buy. Now the tout hesitates, he can either address the Venetiaander family in which case his bargaining position is weakened, or he can not address them. But if he ignores them there is the possibility that they will pass him by and be caught in another spider's web. How does Joseph Italiaander act when he has these two alternatives? He feigns ignorance.

"Hello Mister Venetiaander," he says. "Yes, don't be sur-prised, I know you well because I've seen you walking sometimes with a good acquaintance of mine, Mr. Wagenaar. Nice weather, isn't it? Just taking a little walk with your pretty wife and handsome boy, I suppose. Well, amuse yourselves. By the way, that boy of yours must be about eleven years old so he won't be needing a Bar Mitzvah suit yet for quite a while, I guess.

"Well, never mind, by the time he needs one you should come around."

That shot always hits the mark. Without fail it is the mother who feels hurt and blurts out "Eleven years old? Such a robust boy! Let me tell you that in two weeks he will become Bar Mitzvah, if G'd wills."

After that it's no great feat to keep the fish on the line.

The tout's task officially ends at the doorstep of the shop.
The assistants inside have to take care of the rest of the
deal. Except when the customers are indeed acquaintances
of the tout and want to be helped especially by him.
Someone who wants to buy a piece of textile, for instance,
prefers to be helped by a "meiwe", an expert, a connoisseur. So with a deadpan face the tour tells the shop assistant
"These are special friends of mine. Do you mind if I stay
with them?"

His request is never refused. The shop assistant starts to
show various costumes. Each time, father and mother steal
a glance at their friend the tout, but each time he shakes
his head imperceptibly as if to say "No…"

Of course he doesn't say anything. That's something
father and mother understand very well. After all, he is
employed by the shop so he may not say openly that all
those fine-looking costumes are merely rubbish. When he
finally opens his mouth he says hesitatingly to the assistant,
"Don't you have hanging upstairs that Bar Mitzvah suit the
boss had made for his nephew? You know, he had it made
specially using the finest silks. Pity that when the boy tried
it on it didn't fit him."

The assistant appears to hesitate. "Yes… But I don't
know whether I'm allowed to sell it."

"I will take the responsibility."

The suit is brought down. Father fingers the fabric.
Suddenly he himself has the air of a *meiwe*. "That's good
material. Even a blind man can see that."

"No wonder, first quality worsted, indestructible."

Then the haggling starts. That's part of the game. The
seller asks and the buyer offers half. The assistant says that

he's not allowed to sell it for such a ridiculously low price. Says father "Let us split the difference."

"No, that's really not possible, if the boss hears that I've sold it for such a trifle, he'll fire me."

"If that's the case, the sale is off."

The family stride out of the shop with resolute faces. Firmly they stand in the street. But not too firmly, for at the last moment the shop assistant calls them back. "All right, so have it your way, you can take it for that price. But it is *gonifed* (stolen) for that money…!"

MY FATHER AND MR. LEBOVITZ

My father had a faithful friend whom he called "Mr. Lebovitz". Nobody had ever seen this Mr. Lebovitz, including Father for that matter.

In reality Mr. Lebovitz did not exist at all. He was born in Father's imagination and became a piece of his personality. I can just imagine the birth of Mr. Lebovitz. My father was born a very timid man. He had in his system, however, a very keen sense of judgement about the realities of life and about its problems. "G-d created the world in such a way that everything would come out all right by itself if only people would not interfere," he used to say.

From this philosophical thesis, he tried to explain to his children that controlled indifference is the very essence of the true "art de vivre". But in doing so he constantly had to face Grandmother's opposition, for she tried to govern our household like a tyrant.

I can well imagine how, during one of their arguments as to the proper way of bringing up children, Grandmother might have said, "You are sane and crazy at the same time. How can anybody teach his children a thing like this? When they are grown up, they'll be just the same kind of fools as their father is."

And I imagine that Father probably answered, "A human being should look backwards, never forward. Why should I teach my children that they have to slave and slave and slave? They will spend their lives chasing after themselves. And when finally they reach the finish line and look into their hands, what will they have caught? Nothing."

"*Oy weh*," Grandma lamented, "I would like to know from whom that man always gets those *chochmes*."

And then Father must have answered, "From a certain Mr. Lebovitz…"

"Who is Mr. Lebovitz?"

"Mr. Lebovitz is a friend of mine."

Born as a joke, Mr. Lebovitz became the shield behind which Father hid every time life became too difficult for him.

He could only be himself by putting on the mask of Mr. Lebovitz.

For instance, when he got to bickering with Grandmother, they had noisy conflicts, but not serious ones. Grandmother was bossy and Father resisted by listening in silence. This was more eloquent than a long speech. When he got tired of the flow of words, he would say to Mother, "I saw Mr. Lebovitz this morning."

"What did he say?" asked Mother, understanding and patient.

"Good Morning."

"Nothing more?"

"What more should he have said? When you see somebody every day, you know every word before it is spoken. Silly people just prattle on, but people with brains never say more than what is strictly necessary."

At those words Grandmother would shut her mouth abruptly.

My father was a diamond polisher by trade, like tens of thousands of other working Jews in Amsterdam. Because the diamond industry was hit twice a year by periods of unemployment, periods that lasted six months each time, Father polished more cobblestones than diamonds. Finally, he took up the pushcart with a load of lemons and tried to earn a couple of guilders. When the period of unemployment came in wintertime, he hoped fervently that the whole population of Amsterdam would have to take to bed with flu and drink hot lemon squash. During the summer unemployment, he prayed that a heat wave would come sizzling down from heaven and create a terrific demand for lemon squash with ice.

And what did he report after a typical day of hard work?

"I earned one guilder and a half today."

"Then stop that cursed pushing of the cart," grumbled Mother.

"I saw Mr. Lebovitz today. Next week the entire population of Amsterdam will be running a temperature of 110 degrees."

"Blind Moishe," said Mother.

(Blind Moishe was a character in the Jewish district. If anyone ever said something that the blind man did not believe, he used to say: "Seeing is believing.")

"I bought a stock of ten crates of lemons," said Father. "Mr. Lebovitz says that the prices will rise, so next week I will be a rich man."

Yet, in all honesty, I must admit it seemed that sometimes Mr. Lebovitz could give good counsel. And not only on business matters. Mr. Lebovitz interfered frequently in all our household affairs.

As an example of his influence, let me tell you the story of two girls, sisters they were, in the neighbourhood—in our own rundown apartment building . They lived on the second floor and even as a boy, I realised there was something strange about those two. By day they usually slept but when dusk came, they went outdoors to saunter around, always elegantly dressed. High fashion shoes and, rain or sunshine, white parasols. Their names were Rosa and Dina Sunschein.

"Better—they should have been named Rosa and Dina Moonschein," said Grandmother.

"They are like a pair of owls," added Father. "They never come home before two o'clock in the morning."

"If I were you, I wouldn't take so much notice of those two," interjected Mother.

After she said that, Father did not take notice for a couple of days. But then suddenly, from a chance remark, it became apparent that he had not let the sauntering sisters out of his sight for one single second.

"A man does not walk around with his eyes in his pocket," he would say apologetically. "I see what I see. You cannot blame a man for that."

"Your *shmooz* is good but your arguments are bad," sneered Grandmother.

"Mr. Lebovitz says, 'Just because you love one woman, it doesn't mean you have to hate all other women as if they were enemies,'" Father answered.

"That Mr. Lebovitz of yours is an evil character," Grandmother said.

"Next time I see him, I'll let him know your opinion," answered Father.

If any discussion ever came that far, however, Grandmother wouldn't be satisfied with just ordinary bickering, she wanted a fight. On such occasions Mother intervened.

"How can you be angry about that Mr. Lebovitz?" she asked philosophically. "He does not even exist."

"You are right," said Grandmother with a superior smile. "If you're not careful that husband of yours will drive everybody stark raving mad."

That usually ended the argument. But who had made it come to an end? Mr. Lebovitz of course. He was an extraordinary member of our family.

Everytime anybody talked about the Sunschein Sisters, Father broke out laughing. Mother did not like those two girls at all.

"It is a scandal for the house. Down in the basement, on the ground floor and on the third and fourth floors live quiet, respectable people, if I may say so. But every honest woman would get upset about all that carrying-on on the second floor.

Of course, the neighbours were full of gossip about the Sunschein Sisters. Because they never allowed anyone of us to come into their flat, the tallest stories about them were easily believed. Rosa and Dina, said the know-it-alls, slept in an enormous bed. Their rooms had built-in-mirrors on the ceiling, and in every nook and corner there were lamps with rose-silk lampshades.

The sisters had one friend, one friend together. His name was Mr. Jacobs, and Father said he knew him quite well.

"He is the son of the Jacobs who used to work at Asscher's as a diamond polisher. The father was a small man, you know, and he squinted. The Jacobs who hangs around downstairs is Lowee Jacobs, he's the son of old man Jacobs with the squint. A travelling salesman, he is. No, he is not married, he just likes to go on a spree, now and then. What's wrong about that? When he gets married, he'll have long enough to live in sorrow."

Usually on Friday afternoon, Lowee Jacobs would come to see the sisters. He always stayed until Sunday night. The children of the district got a cent for every errand they ran for him. Buy rolls with beef at Meyer's, buy gherkins at Mouwes', cheese at Berlin's, and pastries at Snatagers', chicken at Heimy Cozijn, and don't forget what they sold at "The Bishops" by the bottle.

"From the money he spends on those two whores, he could run a decent Jewish family with a lot of children," Mother would say.

"If you ask me," Grandmother commented, "he does not earn his money honestly. Anyone who spends it so easily didn't have to work very hard to get it."

Father remained silent. But a couple of days later he would say, "I saw Mr. Lebovitz this morning."

"I suppose he said 'Good morning?'"

"How did you guess? But you will never guess about whom he spoke to me?"

"So—who?"

"About Lowee Jacobs."

Now Mother and Grandmother knew from years of long experience that Father, in a lengthy and roundabout way, would start to relate something for which he could never be held responsible in a formal sense.

"Mr. Lebovitz says that Lowee is a first-class salesman," he announced very seriously. "He may be a little bit on the loose side, but really, he is fundamentally a good boy. That young man spends a lot of money, so what? If he were a miser, you wouldn't like that either."

With Mr. Lebovitz as his reliable spokesman, Father slowly but surely built up Lowee's reputation as a first-class salesman. One night he announced, "I bought something quite new from Lowee today."

It was a sort of special safety pin. Father got a straight-edge razor out of the cupboard. He put that pin on the cutting blade of the razor.

"And now the biggest *schlemiel* can shave himself without tearing the wallpaper from his face," he declared confidently.

"How much did that silly thing cost you?" asked Grandmother.

"At Lowee's, seventy-five cents!"

"Seventy-five cents for a piece of bent wire. I have been wondering for weeks, what is your Mr. Lebovitz after, constantly talking about Lowee. Now I understand," said Grandmother.

"At Kern's in Utrecht Street these things cost two and a half guilders," argued Father.

"Jonas Slap will not like you for this, I don't think," remarked Grandmother tartly…"

Jonas Slap, the barber, lived on the ground floor of our building. He clipped only male customers. In the shop window stood two waxen heads of females coloured with house paint. Jonas was an optimistic man, but he had his worries because a competitor endangered the barber's livelihood. It was the special pin which made the sharpest straight-edge razor as innocent as a shoestring. The invention had recently come from England. Lowee's customers talked wildly about its usefulness but none of them had spent their money on it, up to that point.

"With such a safety pin and your own lather soap and brush, you save all the money you'd normally spend at the barber. Well, of course once every three months you still have to get your hair cut, but you can calculate yourself how much you might save in a year," they told one another.

When Jonas the barber heard that sort of neighbourhood talk, he became very angry.

"Nonsense, those economy gadgets don't exist," he argued.

"Then go to Kern in Utrecht Street to look at a thing that does not exist," they said.

Jonas' aversion to the new invention was generally known and for that reason Father kept silent about his purchase from Lowee. Then came a day when he said he was going to shave his own face for the first time in his life. The whole family sat in the living room around the table, but we took positions so that we could all look into the kitchen. Father covered his face full of white, foamy lather. Then he put the safety razor against his face.

After two very careful strokes, the blood was running down his cheek. He quickly put new soap on that part of his physiognomy. "Mr. Lebovitz says there is no better medicine to stop bleeding than dried up shaving soap," he announced to no one in particular.

Mother said she was afraid that Father would get bloodstains on his shirt. And how do you get them out? Father became very angry. Mother was more concerned about his shirt than about his life. He might bleed to death. And what would she inherit? A clean shirt.

Notwithstanding her level-headedness, Grandmother was somewhat disconcerted by the sight of all that blood. "Shall I go and call the doctor to come?" she asked.

Father, who could not really believe that Grandmother's concern was entirely honest, declared she was teasing him. He locked the kitchen door. Through the door he shouted, "I will shave alone. All your staring and yakety-yak makes me nervous. If you had not interfered, nothing would have happened."

Mother said, "That's what you get when two such floozies live in the same building as yourself. I'd like to drag that Rosa and Dina over the steps like a washboard. If that keeper of those women, that swindling Lowee, had not had you buy that *narrish* piece of bent iron, there wouldn't be a bloodbath in my kitchen right now."

Grandma shrugged her shoulders. "If males are not unreasonable, they wouldn't be anything at all. And that husband of yours, when he can't move forward or backwards, he hides behind that non-existing Mr. Lebovitz."

Time passed. They became restless.

Mother wailed, "G-d knows what's going on in the

kitchen. He may have hit a cheek artery and is bleeding to death!"

"Weeds will not die," said Grandmother.

But as the minutes ticked by, she too became worried. "Even if your husband should become my bitterest enemy for the rest of my life, I must see what is happening in that kitchen. After all, you are my daughter who would become a widow with three half-orphans. We cannot take the responsibility of leaving such a quick-tempered person alone with a razor."

She knocked on the kitchen door. We heard Father move and stumble inside. He did not reply.

"He is still alive," said Grandma. Father's voice rang through the door.

"Mr. Lebovitz asks me to enquire whether maybe you are sorry that I'm still alive?"

After another long wait, he unlocked the door. We all crowded into the little kitchen. He had taken off his shirt and held his head under the cold water tap. All the foam had been washed and wiped from his face. But what a face! One cheek had been shaved. The other one was still black with the stubble of his beard. For that cheek, Father had feared the safety razor was too dangerous. All along the shaven cheek ran a hedge of white cotton batting, dried in the wounds. The contrast made the half-beard seem blacker and the white of the cotton whiter.

Grandma had her comment ready. "A whipped pastry that has fallen on its side in a coal bucket."

"I forbid you to shave yourself any further," commanded

Mother. "If you get blood poisoning, it will be too late to change your ways."

Father looked as if he were put in the corner like a small child being punished. "It's easy for you to say that I may not shave myself anymore, but what can I do? I can't go out in the streets with a half-shaven face," he said nervously.

"You go to Jonas Slap downstairs, let him finish the job."

"I can't do that! Then tomorrow the whole town will know it, and even after a hundred years I won't have heard the end of it."

"Still, you can't go around like that."

"You're telling me!"

After a few moments of silence Mother asked, "What are you thinking about?"

"The same person you are thinking of."

Grandma drew the conclusion: "Lowee Jacobs."

"I'm afraid that's the only solution," said Father.

"I will not let that skirt-chaser come into my house!" cried Mother.

"Well," said Father slowly, "then I will have to go downstairs and ask Lowee whether he will shave me in the flat of Rosa and Dina."

Grandmother resolutely stepped to the door and barred the opening with her body. "Never! You won't leave this room! You'd like that, eh? Fine idea, you going to those tarts downstairs and later telling everybody that your own wife and mother-in-law had sent you."

"And I'll be damned if I go to Jonas Slap's barber-shop in this condition."

"Then let Jonas come here."

"No, that works out the same. He will still trumpet the whole story around."

The solution of the quarrel was that I was sent downstairs with a note. Would Mr. Jacobs please come up. It happened to be Friday, anyway, so Mr. Jacobs was visiting the Sisters. Lowee came, and while he shaved the other side of Father's face, Mother and Grandmother sat at the window staring into the street below like two angry queens, as if Mr. Jacobs did not exist for them.

When Lowee had left. Father showed his clean-shaven face.

"See, not a scratch. The safety thing is first class, but you have to learn how to use it."

Next day a notice was posted in the shop of Jonas Slap.

Self-shavers cannot have their hair cut here.
He who thinks he can shave himself must cut his
   own hair.
We shave only whole faces.
We do not cater to half faces.

(Signed) *Jonas Slap*

That evening, when we sat at the table, Father said, "I would like to know how Jonas got the lowdown about Lowee having shaved the half of my face. Lowee swore an oath that he would not tell."

"I haven't breathed about it to nobody," said Mother.

"You need not look at me," added Grandmother. "I certainly did not tell anybody either. But I know who told Jonas."

"Who told?" Father demanded angrily.

"Mr. Lebovitz, of course," said Grandmother. "Who else but Mr. Lebovitz?"

THE BUILDING

Being a diamond polisher by trade, my father naturally was a member of the Union of Diamond Workers. In our
neighbourhood Henri Polak, the President of the Union
who had worked so hard to improve conditions for the diamond workers, was revered as a miracle-rabbi. Sometimes
this veneration led to ridiculous imitations. Father had a
friend called Sam, a member of the Union Council, who
always agreed with everything Henri Polak had to say in
such a devoted manner that they had given him the nickname "Sam Homogeneous". But Sam considered this a
name of honour. He imitated the way Polak walked and
dressed. He talked and cleared his throat like Henri. I even
suspect that he considered it a homage to himself rather
than to his President, when at the diamond works they
sang one of the Union songs:

> *"When the bosses give us the sack*
> *We turn to Henri Polak*
> *If Henri we should ever lose*
> *We'd be walking on worn-out shoes."*

The Union also made itself felt outside the diamond industry. It did not only strive to improve working conditions

but also did a great job in whipping up an insatiable hunger for the fine arts, especially literature. The simple working people discovered the world of the book.

In the Jewish neighbourhood, Socialism was personified by a man on a bicycle. Nobody knew his real name but everybody called him "Herringhead".

He was the runner of the diamond workers union. He delivered the Union newspaper and collected the subscriptions for the Union Fund that was appropriately called "Help Each Other".

Herringhead was the living link between the organisation and its members. You asked the man on the bike for an explanation when an item in the newspaper was unclear to you. You asked him for advice or aid. Usually he knew the answer, and if he did not, he used to say, "I will ask Henri this week." And then a week later the infallible advice came...Straight from Mount Sinai.

There was only one thing Herringhead could not do, supply the union members with books from the library. If you wanted to borrow books from the Union library on French Lane, you had to go fetch them there yourself. On Tuesday and Thursday night around seven, a small crowd was already standing in line on the high doorstep at the front door of the Building. The library didn't open until eight, but first come, first served. Lezeman, the doorman, was inexorable. Open at eight and not a second sooner. And no pushing allowed, and no loud noises on the staircase.

The library was not just there for lending out books, but also to instruct in the fine arts and sciences. The librarians knew the catalogue by heart. When a young union member enrolled, he was taken aside for a moment and, seated at a table he had to tell the librarian which kind of books he was interested in. Then a list was made up and the librarian saw to it that the young man undertook the great voyage of discovery through the world of the book in a more or less systematic manner.

The library catalogue functioned as a literary guide. By reading these instructive books, the working people sometimes discovered that they themselves had hidden talents, so some of them became actors, musicians, poets, scientists. Others plugged passionately into new arts and crafts and became innovative interior decorators or ceramists.

The craving for beauty and knowledge ran like a torrent over the city. Corporate life started to flourish for people who, until then, had lived in small, closed circles. Self assurance grew, although sometimes this assumed grotesque forms. There were union members who, when they discovered themselves, believed they had made the biggest discovery of the century. Sometimes this led to rather ridiculous incidents.

For instance, our first floor neighbor enjoyed a certain fame for overrating his own importance. He was always running around with bundles of socialist pamphlets, books and newspapers under his arm but he never read one word in them. He only pretended to be a learned man.

Mark Uienkruier (literally "Onionbarrowman") was his name, but everybody called him "*Marx*" Uienkruier. Mark exhibited a morbid preference for alien words. He also had an obstinate inclination to pronounce them incorrectly or to use them in the wrong way. Most stories told about him were probably made up, but the following one is certainly

authentic because he told it to me himself. In fact, he was
very proud of it.

"I had to take my son to the doctor because the little
boy had stomach trouble. So I entered the study of the aes-
culapius and told him "Your honour, my son complains of
pains in the lower part of his abdominal. Will you please
investigate and examine him, for I fear that he is going to
be ill."

The doctor tells me, "Open that lad's fly so I can have a
look at his little thing."

In such a crude and uncivilised fashion that university
man spoke to *me*! I drew myself up to my full height and I
inform him sternly, "Doctor esquire, I am a class-conscious
working man and nowadays our children do not have 'little
things'. My son has a *penis*!'"

Another neighbour of ours, David Augurkiesman
("Gherkinman") was a member of a debating club that
studied political and economic science. Each week the
leader of that club used to assign one of the members to
prepare an essay on some topic or other. The essay was
then read out, and of course, torn completely apart by
the others.

David Augurkiesman was an apprentice in a tailor shop.
It would have been an exaggeration to state that he had the
talent to become a genius in political economics, although
he never missed a meeting of the club. The pathetic thing
about David was that he so much wanted to be an intellec-
tual, but that at the same time he was aware of his short-
comings. His mind moved within the confines of a narrow
room with a low ceiling.

The leader of the club therefore clearly hesitated inviting David to prepare an essay. This made David even less comfortable. But finally one day the leader was forced to ask:

"Now David…Suppose you write down something for next time? What do you say?"

"I shall be delighted," David replied, but from his face you could see that he was none too happy.

"Have you thought about the topic yet?"

"Yes. To tell you the truth, no."

"What would you think," the leader said thoughtfully, "about taking as a topic…Let me see…Yes…The Workers and their Destiny'. Does that subject appeal to you?"

"Sure," David replied, but his voice sounded faint.

"Naturally you are completely free to write what you want," the leader tried to reassure him.

The week passed. David studied and at the next meeting he read out his essay. I can only remember the last part, but I will never forget it even if I live to become a thousand years old. It was the peroration. I remember the words exactly.

"The workers are no longer satisfied with their fate in capitalistic society. Too long they have been forced to eat dry bread. They desire bread and butter, and at least once a week the worker wants bread and bacon!"

"Bread and *bacon*…?" the leader of the club gasped. David Augurkiesman who wanted to eat once a week bread and bacon. *Bacon!* But then a light dawned.

"Hold on, one moment, David," he said. "Where did you pinch that essay from?"

With his face the colour of the party flag, David pulled a crumpled pamphlet from his pocket. It was a propaganda sheet for popularising the Papal encyclical "Rerum Novarum."

Now the club leader was noted for his irrepressible itch to make fun of others at any cost, but this time he managed to control himself... Almost...He only said musing:

"David Augurkiesman and Pope Leo the Thirteenth, how did those two ever get together?"

David made desperate attempts after that blunder to be taken seriously by the study club, but he became more and more uncertain each week. The crisis came when the leader himself presented a magnificent and elaborate lecture on "The Scientific Significance of Karl Marx and Friedrich Engels". Deep philosophical theories, intricate economic doctrines and irrefutable conclusions. The only bright spot in this obscurity of erudition was one short remark— Engels had supported the Marx family financially.

When he had ended, the club members had the opportunity to exchange views with the speaker. David had a question:

"In what line of business was Engels, that he earned enough money to be able to support Marx?"

"He owned a tailor-shop," the learned speaker snarled.

A few days later David terminated his membership of the club. Political and economic science is a difficult field of study...

The Union building was the centre of this splendid movement, the source that fed the large but unified community. Union members regarded the Building as their Temple.

I remember that one night my father took me along to exchange some books. Pointing at the wall of the building he joked "You see that brick over there? The third one in the twelfth row from the bottom? That's *my* brick. It's *our* building, and that one brick is mine."

The architect had equipped the house with a high doorstep so that the person who entered should get the feeling that he had dissociated himself from the workaday world. When the Union celebrated a festival, a jubilee or the introduction of the eight-hour working day, the members expressed their gratitude by presenting gifts for interior decorations.

I remember that one evening my entire family, dressed in festive clothes, strolled over to French Lane. I must have been about twelve years old then. The murals in the board-room had just been completed. The building was on view to union members and their families. In the room a ceremonious atmosphere reigned. The mural paintings, a demure grey contrasting with jubilant green. The furniture, simple but graceful. A table, sturdy oak chairs, a yellow carpet. We viewed more mural paintings in the room where the Union Council held its meetings. On one of them—a man and a woman. Together they read a book. Their hands are joined. And underneath the words of the poet:

"He Read in the Golden Book what Tomorrow will Be." The union members stood waiting in a long line until their turn would come to be guided through the board-room and the council-room. Once inside, they exchanged jokes with the staff and acted jovially with the principals. The women looked first at the paintings and then at the wrought-iron work. Then they turned their full attention to the furniture. They examined the quality of the cloth that lay on the board-table with their fingers. They made critical remarks about the embroidery. Diffidently they trod on the soft carpet. And from their faces you could read that they were thinking "I'm going to make a tablecloth like that too."

With the Union building as an example, a new and handsome style of interior decorating penetrated the living rooms of simple folks. They threw the common oak portrait frames into the fire and they gave the cheap gilt-work from the bazaar to the garbage collector. Instead, they bought reproductions of Da Vinci, which they put behind glass with a simple linen sticker to keep it in place. The place of honour in the living room was reserved for "The Sunflowers" of Vincent Van Gogh. On birthdays they gave each other vases for a present. No living room was complete without an oak panelling. No oak panelling without a row of glazed vases. The women started dressing themselves in terra cotta frocks and black velvet blouses, with a large stoneware brooch as the only decoration. Young men gave their fiancées ornaments of precious metal and wore extra fine silk neckties themselves.

The stream not only gripped the adults, it also carried youngsters towards beauty and renewal. When the doors of the Elementary School closed for good behind them, the youth movement was already waiting outside. There youngsters learned about nature, about flower pistils and stamen, about the birds and the bees. They formed their botany clubs and rambled along the river Amstel to spy on bugs and water beetles in the ditches.

And then a camp was organised…The first camp the youngsters from the Jewish district had ever heard of. A camp with real tents and straw mattresses. Such a thing they had never experienced before. Sleep in tents, just like soldiers, but of your own free will!

Half the neighbourhood stood at the station when the group left. First a photo was taken. I happened to come across it again recently. The boys wear sailor hats that we used to call "ice wafers of a quarter". The girls giggle under straw hats with broad rims.

Nowadays when you walk around the old district, you see ruins everywhere. The old buildings have been demolished or have been put to other uses. The quarter is desolate. The people are gone.

The other day I visited the old building of the diamond workers union again. The lane is now called "Dr. Henri Polak Lane".

The high doorstep.

The revolving door.

But the porter's lodge is empty. Where is Lezeman?

On the hollow-sounding staircase the clamour of shuffling feet and loud voices can be heard. Many offices are established in the building now. Subtenants, they are, nowadays the Union needs only a couple of messy rooms to house its staff. Those few rooms are all that remain of what used to be Our Building.

"We are no more than a shadow of what we used to be," a union staff member told me sadly. "Sixteen hundred members, including the apprentices, that's all we have left. The rest are gone."

In the hall stands the bronze effigy of Henri Polak. The library has disappeared, carried away. By the Germans or their helpers, what does it matter? Completely destroyed.

"Do you still have one of the old catalogues?"

"There's not one left."

"And the booklet with the photos of the murals?"

"One copy we've managed to save."

But thank G–d, the mural paintings have remained intact. The Union had them cleaned recently. Along a back-staircase we went upstairs to the boardroom. The same furniture as in the old days. The same cloth over the table. The same yellow carpet on the floor. And on the walls the magnificent paintings.

"The Strong Hours"—a young man girds himself for the great voyage through Life.

"The Soft Hours"—a thoughtful female figure, a book in her hand.

"The Deep Hours"—a man and a woman lie side by side.

Time moves back. Is it the Present or the Past? Outside, the lane is once more filled with crowds of Union workers. A large figure "8", made of flowers, is hanging out in front.

The people sing:

"Eight hours, resounds through all the lands."

A house full of ghosts, a street full of shadows. The memorial tablet in the boardroom is still there too.

"The apprentices and young members had this board-room fitted as a token of their gratitude and also as a promise for the future, at the *occasion of the introduction of the 8 hour working day.*"

The room is a museum. No, a house of mourning. On that chair, there at the corner of the table, Henri Polak used to sit. Nowadays, when old union members visit the room, they caress the seat of that chair.

The mural painting—A woman lifts a child up from a flower bed. Underneath is written "Oh, to raise our Child towards the Light of Freedom."

And there is the other painting...A man and a woman. Together they read a book, their hands are joined. Underneath are the words:

He read "in the Golden Book what Tomorrow will Be."

MY YIDDISHE GRANDMA

My Grandmother Gittel earned a living for herself and five small children with just a pushcart and some oranges. That was not an easy task because you have to be sharp as a razor in the pushcart business. Eager to get every last cent of profit.

You have to be tough as nails to push that cart around for twenty years through the rain and wind and send your voice climbing up the housefronts. And you've got to be an optimist to believe that people will leave their snug and cosy houses just to buy a few oranges or apples from you. Grandma Gittel was never bothered by false modesty. "Let them imitate what a poor widow has done," she would say proudly.

She herself came from a family of seventeen children. Fourteen died before they were five years old. Grandmother never knew most of those sisters and brothers, yet she said: "We came from a very strong stock. My mother was ninety-nine, and if she hadn't fallen down the stairs, she would still be alive.

If anyone reminded her of the fourteen from that strong stock who apparently had not been so sturdy after all, she would say, "Oh well, sickness does happen."

She was never at a loss for an answer. It always came quickly and usually was to the point. However, sometimes you got the impression that she attached more importance to the swiftness of the reply than to its precision.

Keeping the ritual laws for kosher food, which are quite difficult to carry out, was never any problem for Grandmother. She considered eating pork cannibalism. But she was no synagogue-goer. She used to say, "I worship G-d, not the *shul.*"

Women like her seldom went to the synagogue except after childbirth, for the Bar Mitsvah of a grandson, or when there was a wedding in the family. Yet she taught her grandchildren, "When you find a page torn from a prayer book in the street, you must not throw it away. You should bring it to the rabbi. Throwing it away is a sin in the eyes of G-d."

Grandmother had a leaning towards mysticism; she believed in a force that had something to do with Name. Yes, Name with a capital letter. For that reason the oldest grandson from each of her offspring was named after her late husband, Meyer and woe to any of her children, expecting their first baby, if they considered any other name. She warned, "You may not use a stolen name. It brings bad luck."

"But Meyer is such an old-fashioned name… what if I call the blessed child Max?" Mother had said when I was born.

Snapped Grandma, "So you want them to talk in the synagogue about the 'Five Books of Max' instead of the 'Five Books of Moses?'"

The deep abyss between Grandmother's generation and

that of her children was nowhere more clear than in appreciation of the mystic. She said "If you had seen what I have seen…"

That was a reference to a young man who had been her "steady beau" before she got to know her husband, Meyer, blessed be his memory. That first one must have been a strange fellow, even if I'm convinced that Grandma gradually credited him with more capabilities than he ever possessed. He was born with a "caul", a membrane which sometimes covers the face of a child at birth and is superstitiously supposed to give that person prophetic power. She would picture his appearance—"very plastic", as she put it. "Beautiful, he was decidedly not. No, he was no picture," she used to say.

"There are also ugly pictures," my father consoled.

She snapped back, "You should shut your mouth. If people talk of beauty or ugliness, sons-in-law should be silent. No, I won't say he was a prince, but there was something in his face that you always wanted to look at, but at the same time you wanted to run away from. He was very tall and lean, like a hound. And he had a pointed chin and eyes that changed colour. Sometimes they were dark and sometimes they were light. On each side of his nose he had a wart, right at the corner of his eyes."

She always told us stories about that boy. He could heal children by prayer. How? He prayed and "took" the name of that child and gave it a new one because the "Force", he explained, lives in the "Name". Sometimes in the name of the parents, and in that case he "gave the child new parents", in his way of saying it. So then, with its new name the child got its health back again.

From that boyfriend Grandmother had learned superstitious prejudices against certain foods.

For instance, the evening when Aunt Hannele ran into the streets burning like a torch we had eaten brown beans. And believe it or not, we were also eating brown beans the evening when her brother Lemmi died. After that, no one in our family ever again ate brown beans. Forbidden by Grandmother. It was her magic prejudice. It was all from knowledge she got from her beau.

From that boy also, Grandmother had learned how to predict the future. She did it with the aid of a prayer book and a key. She would go to the darkest corner of the room, behind a door if possible. After tying a cord around the book and making a noose through which she slipped the key, she held the key so that the book could dangle and swing freely. Then she mumbled the magic incantation that she alone knew.

She predicted things to come by observing the way the book swung around. I cannot remember a single case in which her predictions failed. However, I do remember a terrible quarrel between Grandma and one of her step-daughters because she refused to use her magic for predicting the winning number in the public lottery. "My gift may not be used for that," she declared emphatically.

Anyhow, Grandmother had put an end to that friendship after a couple of months because he was so unreliable. Sometimes the boyfriend would disappear for days and when he came back, he would tell her that he had been down deep in the earth or under the sea. And the things he had seen there? Not to be told with two hands.

"Good *schmooz*," grinned father. "Wish I had been born

with a caul. Would I vanish from home now and then!"

When Grandmother was really angry about something, she would announce, "I will throw myself in a fit."

And she did. She dropped to the floor, screaming. At first she did this consciously and deliberately, but after a little while the screams seemed to build up their own power. It was like someone on a swing who gives himself a starting push, then makes the swing arc higher and higher without further help from the ground. That's how it went with those self-made nervous fits of hers. What started as a comedy soon became a drama. Then towels had to be soaked in water and vinegar to wet her hands and forehead. The screaming would subside and after a few minutes Grandma would be completely calm again. Usually her angry mood would have disappeared too.

Her fits were a real nuisance for the family, especially when she came to live with us after all her children were married. Whenever she didn't get her way in something, she threatened to throw herself in a fit. And she could be very troublesome and obstinate. In our house she reserved for herself certain special tasks. She insisted that Mother should leave the cooking of certain dishes to her; she declared that only she could prepare those dishes properly.

Nonsense, Mother said, she could do it just as well but Grandma denied this. "I will throw myself in a fit," she threatened, and that was that.

Smelt, for instance, fried smelt. She insisted that there are small worms in smelt, tiny white worms. And that she had to take these out before the fishes could be fried. Fried smelt she liked to eat, not fried worms.

I don't believe that the white curly marks in smelt are

really worms, but in our household everyone was convinced that they were. The worms had to be niggled out
with a sharp needle while each smelt was held against the
light of a paraffin lamp.

"Then you can clearly see those dirty worms," Grandma
said. Getting the worms out was *her* task. Nobody dared to
infringe on this right. But talking about nervous fits, everybody was on the verge of a breakdown when Grandma sat
for hours on end in the living room, with the paraffin lamp
and the needle and the bunch of raw fish.

The fact is, raw smelt gives off a very penetrating
odour!

Another privilege she reserved for herself was the big
washing. The traditional way of doing laundry in those days
was to cook the dirty linen in a tub on the gas heater. The
boiling lather filled the whole house with the strong smell
of soap. Then the clothes were taken out of the tub and put
into another tub with clean water to rinse out the suds.
Next, piece by piece, the clothes went from that into a
smaller tub standing on a low table. That small tub contained hot soapsuds and a scrub board with a rippled zinc
surface. The laundry was scrubbed until it was spotlessly
clean, and then finally each piece was wrung out by hand,
dried and ironed.

Mother was allowed to do all the jobs connected with
the big wash except the last one, the rubbing and scrubbing
on the board. That was Grandma's duty and privilege. She
had done it all her life. Nobody could do it as well, she told
us. She would not let herself be talked out of that. So each
Monday morning the discussion started in the same way.

Mother asked "Must you stand at the washtub again
tomorrow?"

Grandmother replied with a counter-question, "Are you starting again?"

Then Mother heaved a sigh but said nothing. But her silence really provoked Grandma.

"Why do you sigh? I'd rather you said that you forbid me to do it."

"Fancy anybody forbidding you anything," Mother said sarcastically.

"Naturally," agreed Grandma, "That would be the limit. A child forbidding her mother something. A topsy-turvy world."

Although Mother had promised herself not to become angry, that always got her wound up.

"Even when you are a hundred years old, you will have to be treated like a child. You won't listen to reason. All right, I forbid you to do the scrubbing."

Grandma only shrugged. "Each time I hear the same, 'I forbid you, I forbid you.' Can't you say something different for a change because that 'I forbid you' bores me so."

Then Mother left the room, she had lost the battle. Every Monday she lost the battle, and every Tuesday Grandmother was standing at the tub, with a red head and rolled up sleeves. She did not merely scrub, she fought a war with those dirty cloths. She beat and pummeled the laundry as it were her mortal enemy. When the last shirt had been knocked out, she looked around triumphantly. Once more the family wash had failed to conquer her and she remained the winner.

When Grandmother was getting on into her eighties, Father and Mother decided that the washtub drudgery had to end, even though they might have to drag the old creature away from the tub. Of course they lost. Grandma threatened to go on the balcony with the washing and scrub there, so that the neighbours would think her daughter let her do the wash at her age. And that was that.

The opinion of the neighbours played an important part in Mother's life. Grandma Gittel knew how to profit from that fear. If she thought there was a reason for her to be angry about something, she stopped eating. Then Mother nearly died for shame.

But Grandma did not care for that, in her rather obscure way she enjoyed the sweet satisfaction that the neighbours would think her daughter was starving her to death.

She was a fanatic in this, too. Once she fasted for two whole weeks. During this time she did not eat a single crumb or drink a drop of water. Finally my father called a doctor, and he forced the obstinate creature to eat and drink. I honestly believe she would have fasted to death if she had felt that was the only way to win what she wanted.

But with the same fanaticism, Grandmother Gittel stood guard over her family like a true matriarch of an ancient tribe. Maybe some members of that tribe did not take her sovereignty seriously, but she felt her power undisputed. The family was the only world she acknowledged. Although she had never heard of Ptolemy, she was convinced that her world was the centre of the Universe.

In every family there are quarrels now and then. Grandmother Gittel made herself the judge and arbiter in all our disputes. She would listen, then give her opinion. She had strong sympathies and even stronger antipathies

and for that reason there was always someone in the family
with whom she was not on speaking terms. I have never
known her to budge from a position. But woe to the out-
sider who might dare cause harm to a member of the family. Then all the internal quarrels were forgotten in an
instant and she would fight like a lioness for us. And if I say
"fight" I mean just that, literally.

She had never learned to read or write and her vocabulary was a hodgepodge of Middle-German dialects, distort-
ed Hebrew and Yiddish expressions with, here and there,
like a raisin in the rice, some proper Dutch word. But her
illiteracy never bothered her. Her explanation was simple
and practical, from the old pushcart days.

"I know that an orange which has cost me three cents
cannot be sold for two," she said. "That's all I need to know."

And: "Reading and writing you can learn, but brains
you can only *have*." She never really felt this lack of
knowledge of the alphabet until one of her daughters
moved to London. That daughter wrote letters to the others
in Amsterdam, letters which Grandmother could not read.
She suspected that there was more in those letters than was
read to her. So therefore she had the letters read to her over
and over again. And woe if her suspicious mind suspected
that some phrase did not tally with a previous reading of
the same letter. She had remembered every word.

The neighbours told Mother that Grandma sometimes
came to them with letters from London that she had
sneaked out of Mother's cupboard. Would the neighbours
please read them to her, she had asked? She just couldn't
get enough of them, she explained, but the truth was that
she was trying to check on Mother.

Then that letter came from London in which the daughter wrote, "… in about four months, I expect the baby."

From that moment on, Grandmother became restless. Her daughter was going to have a baby, and she would not be there. Impossible, she told herself, that had never happened before. At all previous confinements in the family, she had assisted the mid-wife. But now her daughter was in a strange land, far from family and friends, and she would not be there to stand at the bedside and tell everybody what was to be done.

So Grandma Gittel made the biggest decision of her life, she herself would go to London. She had saved some money, and it was enough to pay the fare.

My mother objected, "You are utterly meshugah. At your age, a woman in her eighties who cannot speak a word of English. You can't even read or write. They should put you in jail."

Mother called our family together. Grandma sat like a Queen among her courtiers and listened. Everybody spoke at the same time and nobody approved her plan. But they could talk, for all Grandma cared. She only said, "I'm going, and that's that."

And she went, of course. All by herself. The whole family saw her off at the train, as if she were a small child. She had a straw suitcase with some clothes, and bread and butter cake. It was her food for the trip, to live on until she could get food that her daughter had prepared. From strange kitchens Grandmother did not eat.

That was before the First World War, when people could travel between countries without much difficulty. From the train, she transferred to a steamer. She was not a bit seasick either, although the weather was foul during the crossing.

Later she told us a funny story of an encounter she had aboard the boat. In the cabin were a couple of men playing cards, and they asked if she would care to play.

"I told them, 'I will not play for four reasons. The first reason is that I have no money'."

The men said they did not care about the other three reasons. Ha, ha! "Of course, they were card-sharps" she added in case we were not bright enough to catch on.

The ship docked at Harwich, and the customs officer did not bother Grandmother at all. I suppose he couldn't understand the strange language she spoke. She boarded the proper train to London, but there was some misunderstanding so that there was no one waiting for her at the station. There she stood, an old woman quite alone, in the strange metropolis. British money she did not have. English she could not speak. All she had was a slip of paper with the address of the daughter, somewhere in Battersea South. That piece of paper Mother had slipped into her hand at the last moment. What luck! A bobby read the address, and that blessed policeman took her to an omnibus. For hours she sat in the bus, riding through the endless streets. The bus conductor did not bother to ask her for fare money. He only laughed.

"Perhaps, he had never seen a young girl before," Grandma remarked grinning.

Finally, the conductor informed her with sign language that she should get off at the next stop. That slip of paper again. She put it under the nose of a passer by, and the man took her to the house, just a few steps away.

"There was no bell to ring, so I turned the knob and went in, straight to the kitchen and I announced, "Here we are again."

Back in our old neighbourhood, in the meantime, everybody died a thousand deaths waiting for the telegram reporting Grandma Gittel's safe arrival in England. Later, when we told her about our great concern, she explained in a tone that was meant to be casual,

"Well, that's because you don't have travel experience. There was no danger at all. They wouldn't dare kidnap me in broad daylight. And if they had kidnapped me by night, they would have brought me back as soon as they saw me in daylight."

Although she pretended that the journey had been very simple, this modesty was just a sham. In reality, she was very proud of having completed the journey all alone, the more so because the trip was made in the face of disapproval by the entire family.

At eighty-nine Grandma developed a severe pneumonia at the same time that my mother was in bed with influenza. The doctor looked very concerned. "I'm afraid the old woman is going to lose this battle," he confided to us. "True, she is as strong as iron, but pneumonia at that age is practically hopeless. In any case, there should be a trained nurse here," he told Mother sternly. "You sick in bed and your Mother perhaps dying—you must have a nurse night and day."

A nurse came, and as you might expect, Grandmother did not like her. The fault was not with the nurse. Grandma Gittel always had trouble with medical people. She was ill, but that doctor did not prescribe any medicine, she complained.

But if the doctor prescribed something, she refused to take it. The bottle just stood on the corner of the mantelpiece and she did not take a drop.

With the nurse she bickered day and night, despite the high fever she was running. The nurse, that poor helpful creature in her blue-white uniform, really had more than she could do, running from one sickbed to the other.

The doctor prescribed some powders for Mother's flu. Grandmother was also to get some powders. Different ones, of course, for her pneumonia. The doctor warned the nurse against errors.

"Now, for G-d's sake, be careful, before you administer the medicine, be sure to read what it says on the label to see for whom it is. If the old woman gets the wrong powders, you can definitely write her off."

Nobody knows whether the nurse was confused by Grandmother's nagging or what, but she made a mistake. She mixed up the powders and did not discover it until it was too late. Pale as a corpse, the nurse went to Father and confessed her mistake.

Mother had got the powder intended for Grandma, but she recovered from her influenza all the same. She probably would have recovered anyhow without the medicine.

And Grandmother got the influenza powders. So three days later she sat up in bed and ate a piece of boiled halibut. Another week, and she was walking in the streets as usual.

She was not ill ever again until her end at the age of ninety-three.

Grandmother often talked about that powder incident afterwards.

"So that is what happens when you can read and write," she said. "If that nurse had read what was written on those packets, she would have given me the 'right' powder, and you know where I would be now? In my grave."

Yes, my Yiddishe grandma Gittel lived to ninety-three, nearly as old as her own mother, who would still be alive if she had not fallen down the stairs.

In her last years Grandma could not walk so well any more, but her brain remained clear. She would sit at the window in the front room and watch the vendors on the street below loading their pushcarts with produce in the morning. She was at the window again when they came home in the evening, counting how many apples they had left.

"One, two and three is five, and three more is eight…"she would count with them. "He sold 230 apples today. I counted them too when he loaded his cart this morning," she would say.

They say Grandma Gittel died because of a collapse of her physical strength. But I have my doubts. I believe she just did not want to live any longer. I was the last one who saw her alive in the hospital. She was alone in a little room. Quiet, at rest, and perfectly at peace with herself and every-thing. She looked at me with her bright grey eyes.

Her mouth said, "I am going to die. I will be glad to get some rest. I sold all my apples. Now I am going to bring my pushcart home forever. I have finished what I had to do."

The nurse came into the room. It was plain Grandmother didn't like her, she did not like nurses, period… When the girl left, Grandmother said to me,

"If she pays me one guilder, she can have my illness. Believe me, it's a bargain, I paid a lot more to get it." Then she closed her eyes and was dead.

Grandmother Gittel died before the Nazis invaded Holland and, blessed be G-d, she had a grave for herself alone.

WEEKDAYS AND SABBATH

T HE WEEK BEGINS IN THE EARLY DAWN on Sunday morning when the porters noisily carry around the planks and props for the Sunday market. In the first drab rays of sunshine, the empty market booths and stalls arise like spooky gallows from a desolate plain.

At approximately 9:30 a.m. the first customers arrive. Most of them enter the marketplace at the side where an old man who answers to the nickname "Half-a-sleigh" sits in the midst of his old rubbish. Here the discarded trash of an entire continent has reached the end of its journey. How it got here, nobody knows. Half-a-sleigh sits waiting philosophically behind his heap of rusty junk. He is practically blind. All week this little mole has been hanging around in his shed in the alley, waiting for customers. When boys find a wheel or a frame of an old bicycle they bring their stuff to him and ask, "Half-a-sleigh, how much will you give us for this?"

"Two cents."

"Can't you make it three? There are six of us, that's half a cent each."

"Two cents and not a penny more."

"Done!"

Half-a-sleigh buys and takes apart everything. Nuts and

bolts are separated and sorted according to size, thickness and quality. Screws he puts into a bottle, ball-bearings in a wooden box. Then on Sunday morning he moves his heap of rust to the marketplace. If you own an old-fashioned bicycle that still has complicated clock-bearings instead of modern cranks, you can turn the world inside out, but nowhere will you find a spare part except here. Half-a-sleigh feels the broken-down bicycle with his fingers because he can't see it so well, then he says, "Here's the replacement. That will cost you twenty five cents, so you're all right again."

On the other side of the market are the quacks. Doctor Herman impresses his patients with the immaculate white-ness of his doctor's coat. He knows everything there is to know about rheumatic pains. If you have a quarter, you can exchange it for a chip box filled with a greasy substance. Doctor Herman however does not *sell* his medicine, he *gives* it to you as a present, the quarter only serves to cover his expenses. For Doctor Herman's sole desire is to alleviate human suffering, especially the pains that arise due to the accumulation of uric acid in the joints, the formation of bile in the knees, water on the knee which affects the heart, and chronic gout in another part of the human anatomy which he will not name because there are also some children standing around listening. The doctor makes no secret of the fact that his medicine is basically lard with a drop of oil and gin added. But it also contains a certain mysterious component which is his special secret.

He tells, "My whole family uses it, and that I consider the biggest miracle of all. But now I will tell you another miracle. The other day I got rheumatic pains myself. Here, in this left arm of mine. I couldn't lift it. So I went to my family doctor. 'X-ray treatment,' that learned man tells me. But X-rays don't help. 'Go to a specialist' another doctor tells me. So I visit the professor. He examines me, he carries out a telephone conversation with my heart. He taps on my chest and my back. Finally he says 'You are perfectly healthy and you owe me twenty five guilders.' I give him the banknote but the pain in my arm remains. He scribbles some Latin on a scrap of paper. If you please, ten guilders for the Chemist. But I still cannot move my arm. Then my wife says to me 'You know what you should do? You should rub some of the rotten concoction of your on that arm.' I reply, 'You are meshugge, that stuff is for my customers, not for me. Do you think that Rabinowitz the pastry-cook eats his own cakes?' But you know how these things go, when you are in pain and you want to run up a wall in order to get rid of it. Finally, I let my wife have her way. I rub that stuff on my own arm and lo and behold, the next day the pain is gone. See it for yourself, here, this arm which I couldn't move… Now I can move it in a normal way. Costs only one quarter…

Next to Doctor Herman is the stand of two brothers, Jacob and Marcus. The first is a specialist in the treatment of corns, the other has spent his life studying toothaches.

The secret of Jacob's medicine for corns is a pain-killing ointment which he spreads on the patient's toes. He tells him "Take of your shoes, mister."

"Yes."

"Now take of your socks."

"I've taken them off already."

"Oh, I thought you still had your socks on."

Jacob spreads the ointment on the painful spot. "We'll let the medicine soak in. Now come here. See, the pain is gone."

The doctor steps with his shoes and all, and with his full weight on the bare corn. The patient keeps smiling, he feels nothing.

While the nature of Jacob's medicine for corns is simple to understand, the toothache cure of his brother Marcus has an air of mystery around it. The toothache powder is dissolved in water and forms a milky liquid which clots in the mouth of the patient.

"Have you rinsed your mouth thoroughly?"

Marcus jumps down from his stand. He snatches a cap from the head of a bystander and presents it to the patient.

"Spit in here."

Marcus searches with a pair of tweezers in the pulpy spittle. "There you are, here are the toothache bacteria. Your pain has disappeared, has it not?"

"You're right! I don't feel anything! The pain has gone!"

The toothache bacteria are visible to everybody. From a distance they look like pulpy threads or fibres.

A little further on, the street-singers earn their living by singing lilting songs of drama and romance. One of them accompanies himself with his concertina and tambourine.

> *"He kisses her lips*
> *But she whispers low*
> *You must desist*
> *Please my dear, be slow.*

But he kisses again
And he feels her give in
And he cannot stop
In their hearts it is Spring."

A few feet away, Mozes the escapologist lets himself be tied up with a chain, a thick rope and a padlock. He offers twenty-five guilders to anyone who can manacle him in such a way that he cannot free himself within three minutes. Any kind of knot is permitted. Every Sunday, all the year round, the same man tries in vain to win this twenty-five guilders prize. However, his friendship with Mozes does not appear to suffer appreciably from his futile perseverance, for one can often see them together, drinking a glass of beer.

Further on again are the second-hand bookstores. Potential buyers browse among these old editions. Take your pick! The third volume of *World History* by Streckfuss, one of twenty-four volumes, the other 23 still wander through the Diaspora. A hand grabs a book with a yellow cover with red lettering: *Le Livre de l'Amour de l'Orient.* The man lets the book drop again at once—The French is wasted on him.

Although some folks seek the aid of quacks on the market, most inhabitants of the district go to a regular doctor for their medicine. On weekdays at 7 a.m. the waiting room of Doctor Lamb is already crammed to overflowing. Half the district is his patient. The doctor knows everything about every family, whether business is good, how much money is earned, about marriage problems of a very personal nature. Sometimes he is a mediator at engagements and marriages, and intercedes at small business transactions.

On the wall of his waiting room hangs a poster showing a doctor examining a gaunt little boy. It says:

> *"That's right, Mother*
>   *Have your child examined before it is too late."*
>   *On another sign it says:*
> *"Washing is good*
>   *Bathing is better."*

Although he is a great admirer of scientific progress, Doctor Lamb is also a cautious man, he only uses the methods that he learned as a student. His prescription for all affections of the chest and lungs is invariably to stick your head in steam coming from a boiling kettle.

His patients hasten to obey for they have a deep-rooted fear of being operated on. For generations they have been taught that the human body is a holy temple and that one may not rashly cut into a holy thing. But sometimes an operation is so urgent that even Doctor Lamb dares to hesitate no longer.

"You have to be helped, I'm afraid. But they put you under an anaesthetic, and when you wake up you will have noticed nothing."

To cheer up his patients he tells them funny anecdotes. "Last week I was visiting an old woman and I asked her 'How is your stool?' She replies, 'Not very rosy, doctor!' Ha, ha, ha. But yesterday I asked a woman patient, 'how is your stool' and she answered 'You are sitting on the only stool in the house.' So I say again 'No, I mean, do you have suffi-cient bowel movement?' And she says 'Well, doctor, a mouthful now and then.' Ha, ha, ha!"

Doctor Lamb is a keen judge of character, his insight in psychology has furnished him with certain secret medicines. For instance, when he has to visit a particularly gloomy patient, he asks an organ grinder to play on his street organ in front of that patient's house. Then Doctor Lamb arrives. He knocks on the patient's door. When he enters the room she is lying in bed looking at him mournfully.

"Good day to you, Mrs. Stein. And how are you today?"

"Ach doctor, I'm afraid I am finished. What can I tell you, my legs are stiff and my arms are racked with pain. My back aches and I have stitches in my behind. And I myself don't feel so good either."

Says Doctor Lamb "Let us begin by opening the window."

Through the open window they hear the music of the street-organ. Then Doctor Lamb becomes merry, he starts to waltz around the room.

"Ta-ta-ta, ta-ta-ta…"

After a few steps he says "My dear, come out of bed. Let us waltz together. I do so want to dance with you, Mrs. Stein."

In nine out of ten cases the woman gets out of bed and waltzes with Doctor Lamb around the little room. Usually she is cured the same day of her dreadful disease.

While they sit in the doctor's waiting room, the patients chat among themselves. In the course of their conversa-tions they sometimes discover that they are distant relatives.

The art of finding out whether you and the other person belong to the same family (mishpocheh) is called "mish-pochelogy".

I will give you an example of this science.

The conversation starts as follows:

"I am a Pereira."

"Then you are of Portugese parentage? In that case you maybe are mishpocheh of Sal Pereira who used to live near Amstelveld?"

"I know who you mean. Sal Pereira, who was married to Abraham Pereira da Costa da Fonseca, she was a daughter of Isaac Levison who walked with the *chewrebook*, his mother was a Herschel, her husband was a Salmonson, Benny Salmonson. Och, you must know him, he had a big schnozzel, Benny Schnozzel we always called him. No, he is no relative of mine, I am a Goldstein, my husband is a Pereira de Salzedo, not just Salzedo, but *de* Salzedo."

"Then is he one of the Salzedo's who used to live in Weesper Street in a cellar where they have a cigar shop?"

"Exactly. Now you've got the right one."

"Well, will you believe it when I say that we are of the same family? My uncle Jossie, Jossie of Mitzi, they live in Swan Street right opposite baker Con, well this Uncle Jossie is married to one Salzedo who used to live on Breestreet and who is a niece of the Salzedo of Weesperstreet."

"You mean Raatje of Jossie of Mitzi? Oh, yes, I know her. That is family of mine, her mother and my mother are nieces."

"Is her mother still alive? She must be nearly eighty."

"Eighty? She is ninety-four, unbeschrien unberufen, ninety-four!

"Is that so? Well, then she is not listed anymore on the Bingo numbers."

Bingo evenings are the highlights of family life. In the Jewish quarter of Amsterdam everybody plays Bingo. Every evening. In all the families, wealthy or poor, they play Bingo.

After supper, when the dishes have been washed and a pot of tea is standing ready on the table, someone says "Let's play Bingo."

"All right, you fetch the boards."

"Who will call the numbers tonight?"

"I will do it."

Playing Bingo in the Jewish district is a game for intelligent people. The numbers are called by their nicknames, and these you have to know by heart if you do not want to go wrong. If a player cries out that he has won, and it turns out that he has filled in a wrong number, he hides his head in shame. Bingo sharpens the mind because it develops a feeling for intonation and charade.

Everybody knows that Number One is called the *Pisher*, the bed-wetter or little squirt.

And you do not have to be a genius in order to understand that the *Little Swan* is Number 2. So naturally, *Two Little Swans* is 22.

But what is a *Yiddish Hatchet*? You don't know? Then look at the shape of Number 7.

The game becomes more complicated when Number 6 is taken out of the bag. The caller chants "Mr.Bottleman!"

Oy, who is Mr.Bottleman?

Mr. Bottleman runs a millinery shop in Saint Anthony Street. Everybody knows this. But what has that to do with

Number 6? The solution is simple. With some imagination you can see that Number 6 has the shape of a bottle.

However, there are also difficult call-names which are based on the fact that in Hebrew the numbers are designated by letters. Every word in Hebrew is therefore not only a combination of letters but also has a certain numerical value. For instance, in Hebrew the letters of the word *kouach* add up to 28. Kouach means strength. Who had strength? Samson. In Hebrew: Shimson. What was Shimson? A hero and a strong man, *Gibour* in Hebrew. So when the caller chants "Shimson-the-gibour…" you know that he means 28.

In the same way *mazel tov* (good luck) stands for 49. It is a kind of Caballa. In this way, every number has a name. The 8 is called the pretzel, Number 12 is called "good afternoon" and Number 13 is the Bar Mitzvah Boy. Number 44 is named Chanukah because that feast lasts 8 days, and two times 4 is 8. The highest number, 90, is The Old Man.

Some Bingo players have a legendary fame as callers and at Bingo games they are the guests of honour. They are invited everywhere, one night here, the next evening somewhere else. But not on Friday nights, for on Friday the Sabbath begins.

The *shabbesmachers*, Sabbath makers, always make their rounds on Friday and they appear just before the Sabbath begins. That time changes every week. When the Sabbath starts early, for instance at 4:30 p.m., the shabbesmachers appear in the streets at 4 o'clock. Then, at 4:30 they have disappeared again. On the other hand, when *shabbes* starts late, the shabbesmachers also appear late. So it is just as if they "make" the Sabbath, and that is why they are called Sabbath makers. They walk up and down the streets and alleys singing their songs. From the windows, coins wrapped in paper, fall down on the pavement. They are gifts from the Jews preparing for the Holy Day.

When the last shabbesmacher had left, the expectant tranquillity of the Friday evening descends on the neighbourhood. The day of rest has begun. The streets are deserted. Behind the closed curtains the lamps are burning. The families are gathered around the table covered with a white cloth. Generation after generation sat like this, for hundreds, nay thousands of years.

And every Friday night again there is that moment of expectation, the second of motionless quiet, before the meal begins.

Through the thin wall one can hear the singing and praying of the neighbours. Age-old melodies. A few hours later, when the tables have been cleared, the light behind the curtains are dimmed. Silence reigns everywhere. It is as if a large glass dome has been put over the old district which cuts off all sounds.

The repose of the night is followed by the quiet of the Sabbath morning. No noises on the streets. No creaking of carts. No children who have to go to school. Only some pious men who shuffle to the *shul* carrying under their arm the velvet bag with the prayer shawl.

The long and venerable Sabbath continues and goes on and on, until the first star appears in the sky.

And then the week begins anew...

Marken Alley, where the author Meyer Sluyser was born in 1901.

The Jewish Broad Street (Jodenbreestraat) on the eve of a holy festival.

Burning the ritually unclean bread on the the day before Passover.

The heart of the old neighborhood.

Fish seller.

Early Sunday morning in the Joodse Houttuinen ("Jewish Woodgardens".)

Seller of horse-radishes.

Jilenburg ("Owlburg".)

Mr. Cocadorus, the comical market vendor.

The market on Sunday morning.

The market on Waterloo Square.

Market women. The writing on the wall says: D.L. de GOEDE
("The Good") MERCHANDISE in ALL SORTS of SALTED, SMOKED
and DRIED FISHWARES Whole Sale and Retail the CHEAPEST
address on this street.

kins of hares and rabbit are hanging on hooks in the entrance of this
hop which bears the sign "We buy Rags and Bones and Metal Wares."

A "Water and Fire" shop where the women from the district bring the household feces.

Removing sewage. In the Jewish neighborhood the van was mockingly called the "fee marriage."

The beginning of the end. The sign put at the entrance of the Amsterdam
Jewish district by the Nazis closing it off before the inhabitants were
deported and murdered in the concentration camps.

ABOVE Buying matzoth (unleavened bread) in Valkenburger Street.

RIGHT Exhibition on the streets of Amsterdam of photographs of the old Jewish quarter and excerpts from Meyer Sluyser's books. The exhibition was organized by the Municipality of Amsterdam on May 5th 1990 on Jonas Daniel Meijer Square in the center of the city to commemorate the 45th anniversary of the liberation of Holland by Allied forces on May 5th 1945. The Portugese-Israelite synagogue built in 1671 can be partly seen in the background.

The author Meyer Sluyser.

DISPUTES

HYDEPARK CORNER, IN LONDON, is known all over the world because there you can climb onto a soapbox and blurt out to the world whatever you want to say. But did you know that in Amsterdam there used to be not one, but *two* Hydepark Corners? One was on the Amstelveld on Monday morning, and the other was on the New Market on Saturday night.

The know-it-all's who have been smitten with Leon Tolstoy's pipe-dream that the world wants to be improved, mount their hobby-horses on the Amstelveld in the morning around 10:30 a.m. However, before that hour some early birds already hang around the market. Their only purpose to be there is to disagree with the speakers, but while waiting for their opponents to appear they wander around the stalls and listen idly to the sales talks.

A salesman demonstrates the marvels of a mysterious liquid substance which makes spots and stains disappear from silk in no time at all.

"See it for yourselves," he shouts. "I dip this piece of silk in the spirits of salt. It fades, it becomes blue. The caustic bites into the fabric. I'll have to throw it away, you think.

Worthless it has become, you tell your wife. Wrong, wrong, wrong! Here, let me show you…I take the stain remover, I add a few drops of water to it, I brush it like this over the spoiled piece of silk, and what sees my ear, what hears my eye, what runs my nose, and what smells my foot…? There, the original colour has come back. See it for yourself, Mister, costs only one quarter, twenty-five cents!"

A few steps further on, a man is standing behind a tall water column. Through the glass in the top of the column a small doll can be seen floating in the water. That doll is "Tiny Thomas". He can tell the future, Tiny Thomas can. You have to buy an envelope from the man and make sure that there's a blank piece of paper inside. When you've paid him, the man places the empty sheet beneath the water column.

"Tiny Thomas is still upstairs," he shouts, "but when your letter lies under the column, Tiny Thomas comes downstairs. He thinks for you, he sees the future of married and unmarried persons, of old and young, of rich and poor!"

As though moved by magic power, the doll sinks to the bottom of the column. Its thinking process takes only a couple of seconds, then Tiny Thomas rises back to the surface, swift as an arrow. Look, look! The blank sheet is now covered with writing! In a clear scrawl a person can read what the future tried to keep hidden from him.

The early birds however have not come to watch stains disappear from silk, they want to remove the stains that cling to Capitalistic Society. True believers they are, not in Tiny Thomas but in Prince Peter Kropotkin who has explained in a book how the workers should take possession of their daily bread. The Amstelveld becomes lively when Sourbeer arrives, preceded by an empty beer-barrel which he rolls along by every now and then kicking it with his foot. That barrel is his pulpit. Sourbeer is an anarchist. He has eyes blue as forget-me-nots, the voice of a chaste spinster and the vocabulary of a dock-worker, the amiability of a rattlesnake and the tolerance of a head-hunter. He speaks undiluted Amsterdam slang, his metaphors are more daring than those of Fockenbroque, his dislike of the police, the Queen and the Royal House of Orange is boundless. He is an atheist with a negative religion, because he rails at a G-d who doesn't exist. In his mincing voice he crows:

"The other day a lady was standing before me barrel and suddenly she says 'Sourbeer', she says, 'they've pinched me bag. Look, they've cut it off at the handle clean as a whistle. Me purse was inside with all me housekeeping money, and oh Mister Sourbeer', she says, 'What shall I do. Shall I go to the coppers and claim damages?'"

So I answer 'Woman,' says I, 'if they've cut off your bag the last thing you should do is to go to the cops because they will pinch the straps as well. But don't be sad, you would have lost your housekeeping money anyway because She of the Royal Family has to have a raise again, they can't make both ends meet. So now we have to fork out for the Royal House, yes ma'am. You may declare that there's a housing shortage, but I can name you a house that badly needs to be cleared away first, and that is the Royal House."

Sourbeer interrupts his cursing to poke fun at his neighbour, missionary Baas, who is talking from atop a soap-box a couple of feet away. "That shmoe over there did his exams in Theology the other day," he crows. "I know, because I sat next to him in the sweating room when he had to go to the Professor. The student who is before him was put a question, the Professor asked him 'My son, what wouldst Thou do if Thou wert in the wilderness to preach the Gospel to the heathens and a fly comes and settles on your nose?' Says the student 'I would shoo it off gingerly, because we must extend love to all living creatures.' Then the Professor says 'You're an idiot because that fly may give you sleeping sickness. No, you have to take that sonofabitch between your thumb and forefinger, squash him and send him to his eternal salvation.'"

Well, then it was the turn of that fellow over there. Asks the Professor 'My son, what wouldst Thou do if Thou wert in the wilderness to preach the Gospel to the heathens and Thou cometh face to face with a lion?'

Says that shmoe 'I would take him between thumb and forefinger, squash him and send him to his eternal salvation.'

So he failed for his exam because he was too dumb to preach to the savages in Africa, but for the Amstelveld on Monday morning he's good enough."

Sourbeer lives mainly on the sale of "*De Socialist*", the newspaper of anarchism in Holland. However, he only has very old issues in stock which he has got hold of for practically nothing and sells for fancy prices.

Another star debater is a hefty dock-worker who for years has been constantly trying to demean himself in the eyes of his fellow men. The reason for his self debasement is a much-fingered pamphlet by Max Stirner entitled "The

Individual and his Property." He proclaims:

"Everything I do springs from pure selfishness. That is because Egoism is the only motive of human action. Never have human beings done anything except for self-gain."

The bystanders listen attentively but for one little Jewish fellow this theory goes too far. After all, he stems from a people for whom *rachmones*, compassion, is considered the highest virtue. So he cannot keep silent.

"How can you say something narrish like that? Everything a man does he does out of egoism? Meshugaas! Imagine that I walk over that bridge over there and I see you lying in the water of the canal. Well, just in a manner of speaking of course, because I hope that you will live to be a hundred. So I see you in the water, you are drowning. I cannot swim, but what do I do? I jump anyhow, wham, over the railing and into the canal to get you out. I nearly drown, myself. If other people who *can* swim hadn't pulled both of us out, we would have cycled on a tandem together to Heaven. Now will you please explain to me why I risked drowning out of egoism? Oy, if I had really been an egoist I would have stayed on the bridge, wouldn't I? But I had real rachmones with you being a corpse, so to say."

The bystanders murmur in agreement. The logic is crystal clear, the example convincing. But the dock-worker does not give up so easily. "No Mister, you're wrong. Let us analyse what you thought when you jumped in after me. You were strolling happily along the street. You reach the bridge at the end of the street and suddenly you hear someone crying for help. You look down and what do you see? You see me lying in the water drowning. That is a terrible thing to see. Your pleasant thoughts are chased away.

You cannot stand the sight of my corpse, so what do you do to get rid of that terrible vision? You jump into the water…From egoism, simple and pure, because you want to erase that vision from your mind. You do it for yourself, not for me."

The little fellow answers "You are making a mistake there, and not a little one either. If you'll pardon me, I will follow your thoughts for a while. You say I am walking happily along the street? Right, I am strolling along happily, thinking of the chicken-soup I will be eating this evening because today is Friday. So far, so good. Suddenly I hear shouting and I see you lying in the water. You are a terrible thing to see, you are telling me? Fine, nobody knows that better than yourself. So far I agree with you. But then you say that in order to escape from the terrible sight of you, I jump into the water? Why should I do that, why on Earth would I jump into the water? Either you are meshugga or you don't know me. Why should I try to save you, I can't swim, can I? You know what I will really do, I will hurry away as quick as I can. In that way I can escape from the terrible sight of your corpse. Do you know what else? I'll call out to other people 'Who can swim? There's someone in the water!' That's what I'll do. Even if I am an egoist, I'm not crazy."

Says the apostle of Stirner "You are twisting my example around. In my example you do jump into the water and you do it out of egoism."

Says the little man "Then you will have to find yourself another example. I know how I am, better than you. You are trying to talk me into being an egoist and I won't accept that!" Looking insulted he pushes through the crowd while commenting "That fellow hates himself but as a matter of fact he's as much an idealist a I am. Oy, so why does he make himself out to be a wild beast?"

Next to this circle another crowd is gathered around Cohennetje (little Cohen) who lectures the masses on the intricacies of Sex. He is a small, slim fellow with a face like a pear drop and wears a pointed hat, a loose tie with flaps, and a cape. At his feet is a gunnysack. What professors at the university do not know yet of Sex, has already been revealed to him. All by himself he assaults sacred cows. But he does not stop at words, he brings his theories into practice. His consistent attitude has landed him in jail many a time. But as soon as he is out he addresses himself to the masses again. For Cohennetje can't keep his mouth shut, when he doesn't do time, he talks.

The gunnysack contains a red and a white cabbage. This is because Cohennetje has discovered that among red and white cabbages there are sexual distinctions. There are male red cabbages and female red cabbages. Some white cabbages are ladies, whereas other white ones are gentlemen. But—and this is the brilliant discovery of Cohennetje—once per so many cabbages the sexual characteristics are a bit mixed up. In that case you find a red one which is both boy and girl. Or you have a cabbage which all by itself possesses a kind of "third sex". After he convinced himself of these truths, Cohennetje has gone out to teach humanity that in the field of sexuality, no aberrations or exceptions exist, because everything is arranged in, and by Nature.

"Everything in Nature is normal. Only the secret desires are the natural desires!"

One bi-sexual red cabbage can convince humanity quicker than a thousand words. Therefore, Cohennetje searches everywhere for singular cabbages. He is a dauber by profession, but the main part of his small income he spends at the green-grocers. Standing amidst his auditors he shrieks in his falsetto voice "Sir, will you please look at this cabbage for a moment. This one is normal, it is a female white cabbage. You can tell by the way the heart has grown, those things over there are the female organs. And this red cabbage is male, just look, the organs are in the same place but now they are masculine. Beautiful, those lines, don't you agree? Now look at this cabbage, there, male and female both together. And this cabbage is again different."

The bystanders study the vegetables with solemn faces, what their eyes see their minds must believe. Cohennetje shrieks hysterically "And because I lead my life according to Nature's truth, just like the red and white cabbages, that's why class-justice throws me in the clink! A human being is worth less than a vegetable."

The discussion now moves quickly away from sexual problems and turns into a heated debate on the class-character of the judiciary. The debates on Amstelveld are kept strictly within the boundaries of hazy speculation.

Genuine contemporary politics are more the business of the New Market on Saturday nights. A dark sky arches over the blackest neighbourhood of Amsterdam. The wavering white light of carbide lanterns casts an imitation moonlight over the pickled herrings, cigars and steel-wares. In the darkest part of the square, the old town weigh-house, you can find the push-carts and stands of the world reformers. The contours of the old weigh-house, where long ago criminals were hung, stands out against the luminous glow coming from the Red Light District nearby. From there the singing resounds of the band of the Salvation Army, marching out to save souls who do not want to be saved. From further on one can hear drinking songs and in the narrow alleys boys and girls make love. The voice of a reciter drones over the market.

> *"Like a roaring fire in the August sun*
> *Storms and dashes the Second Squadron*
> *And we stare after it as it rushes on."*

It is a poem about the second squadron of the cuirassiers of Canrobert, which was machine-gunned, like all the other squadrons in fact, to the last man. This not only decided the outcome of the Franco-German war of 1870, but was also an argument, used by pacifists, to stop all wars because the cuirassiers of Canrobert might just as well have remained quietly in their barracks. Nobody on the New Market needs convincing that the highest vocation of Man is to be a human being, that is to say, an anti-militarist. They only disagree among themselves about the quickest way to bring about the new society. The dynamiters dream of a bomb under the Royal Palace. The philosophers argue that militarism will cease to exist as soon as everybody will ignore its existence. Others have an in-between view, they want to demolish the barracks, break the guns in two, and chase away the regiments.

Nearby lie the Jewish neighbourhoods. The inhabitants with their fierce interest in public affairs long to free all slaves from the capitalistic Egypt. They dash into the fray with the pointed rapiers of their oratorical talents. Among them are Christian-socialists, free-socialists, revolutionary-socialists. There are anarchists and free-anarchists, anarcho-syndicalists and ordinary syndicalists, there are Tolstoyans and Lutherans (the latter are not the followers of Martin Luther but of Barry Lutheran).

The Jewish debaters have studied the subtle art of dialectic oratory from three-cent pamphlets. They are utterly self-confident, their insight in history gives them strength. Their Christian opponents have historical insight as well, but unfortunately their history does not go so far back...

HOW ZELIK MISSED OUT ON TWO INHERITANCES

*I had an uncle called Zelik who in later years everybody consid-
ered a little bit meshuga. That was because he couldn't stop telling
everybody how in his youth he had let two big inheritances slip
through his fingers. This is how he told the story to us.*

MAYBE YOU THINK THAT I AM LYING, but it's as true as the
Good Lord that in my youth I missed out on two jerushos,
two inheritances worth, together, maybe a million guilders.

Well now, perhaps a million is a little exaggerated. So let
me play it safe and say half of that. I know you're still scep-
tical even at that cut price, so I'll make it as low as possible.
Call it two inheritances amounting together to one hundred thousand guilders. That's how much got away from
me. Yes, from me, Zelik. And why did all that money walk
away right out from under my nose? That's what I am
going to tell you now.

I had two aunts, both really exceptional women, I must
say, and between them there was never a bad word; only
they couldn't stand the light in each other's eyes.

Not that they were what you'd call sworn enemies, not on your life. My two aunties went around with each other all right, but if I tell you that they couldn't get along together, then I mean that Aunt Pessie was jealous of Aunt Breinie and that Aunt Breinie simply couldn't sleep from envy of Aunt Pessie.

What's the one thing women always do to pick each other's eyes out? They use their husbands, of course! But Aunt Pessie and Aunt Breinie were both married to real wide-awake sleepyheads so they were equal as far as that was concerned. So, what else can women use to try to out-play each other? Well? Money, naturally. But both of my aunts were what you could call well-off financially, and about equally so. So what was there left for them to pester the life out of one another with? Well? Just plain bragging and out-trumping each other with their talk about their riches and trying to out-buy each other, that's what.

I'm sure you wonder how anyone in our family hap-pened to come by so much money. You want I should teach you something? *Mazuma* is only a matter of brains, because whoever is born for a penny never comes in for a dollar. Let me tell you a story to make my point. When we Jews danced around the Golden Calf in ancient times, Rabbi Moses got so mad that he broke the tablets of the Ten Commandments into little pieces. Anybody can now read about that in the Holy Torah. But what isn't written there is that the Jews, for punishment, had to keep all these pieces of the shattered stone tablets. That's what we've been carrying around all over the world for centuries.

When the pieces first got doled out among the Jews, the rich Jews got the pieces on which was written "Thou shalt…"and the poor parychim got the pieces with "Thou shalt not…" You follow me? Good! So it came to pass, that both Aunt Pessie and Aunt Breinie got a big piece on which was written with letters of gold "Thou shalt". That's how rich both of them were, and they were jealous of each other, as I maybe told you already.

If Aunt Pessie bough a new lamp for her front room, then Aunt Breinie had to buy two new lamps, one for the front room and one for the back room. If Aunt Breinie had her chairs upholstered in velvet, then Aunt Pessie couldn't be happy until her chairs were covered with velvet and gold ribbon. When no more lamps could be bought, no more furniture upholstered, no more carpets spread, Aunt Breinie discovered something brand new to show off the money. And what was it? She went abroad, that's what!

In those days, people did not go on vacation. Vacation, that is a newfangled idea. In the old days, if people had some free time, they went out of town. And where did they go? To Haarlem and Zandvoort; to Arnhem and Nijmegen; to Alkmaar and Bergen; to The Hague and Scheveningen; they were always going to two places at once, but both of them in Holland. But not Aunt Breinie—she went with her Sjaje for a little trip along the river Rhine. And she sent the whole world picture post-cards from the Rhine. Naturally Aunt Pessie got the most beautiful one of all, with mother-of-pearl on the mountains. And on the card was written: "Dear Pes, Sjaje and I are standing here on a mountain, such a high mountain you just can't imagine how small a human being is, nothing but a pile of horse manure; your cousin Breinie."

Naturally, Aunt Pessie was beside herself with anger, and

it got even worse when Aunt Breinie came back from the Rhine and for weeks afterwards was everywhere and all the time walking around humming:

> *Oh, a trip along the Rhine, Rhine, Rhine,*
> *Is so lovely and so fine, fine, fine,*
> *In a pleasure boat so dear, dear, dear,*
> *Glass of beer, beer, beer,*
> *Glass of beer, beer, beer…*

It was not actually humming and it was not exactly what you could call singing, but it was sheer torture for Pessie, and the whole family knew that Aunt Pessie had to do something to get back.

But what could she do? What nobody thought about, is what she did. With her husband, Sakkie, she went to Paris! For fourteen long days the whole world got the most scandalous picture postcards from her, with naked girlies on them and now and then a scene of the city. Special for Aunt Breinie she sent a letter full of French words, which I don't remember except that I do know that one thing it said was "In Paris the traffic is so bad that one horse walks with his nose against the backside of the horse in front of him."

Then, when Pessie got back home, she deafened our ears with stories about a Yiddish family from the Rue de Peeyay, and she tossed around French words that she had learned from those people. Well, how could Aunt Breinie top that? I'll tell you right away.

Those were the days when huge sideboards were coming into style, so Breinie had her front parlour cleared out.

Then she hauled in an oak sideboard with curlicues and twisted legs and gleaming locks and statues in the what-not, and the whole street came to look at this splendid furniture specimen.

Exactly fourteen days later, Aunt Pessie also had her living room emptied. Up to her front door drove an enormous furniture van with six horses, and what did it bring? Also a sideboard. Not any bigger than Aunt Breinie's, but made completely of polished mahogany. She had to have a cleaning woman come one day extra every week just to wax and shine up this magnificent sideboard.

What did Aunt Breinie do then? She bought crystal, a vase and then another vase and a *pièce de milieu* and a crystal dish for small calling cards and another for large calling cards and silver frames for the portraits and porcelain statuettes; and there was too much junk to be taken care of. Of course, Aunt Pessie was also buying crystal vases and dishes and silver frames, until the family agreed they were even again.

But Aunt Pessie was also doing something completely different. What I am now going to tell you, I know you may not believe. But may I never have another healthy hour if one single word of this is a falsehood.

Try to guess what Aunt Pessie was about to do? No, don't waste your time, it just can't be guessed.

Aunt Pessie had some cards made, and on these cards she wrote the prices of the vases and the dishes and the silver frames. Next she placed the cards on her mahogany sideboard. It was a perfect showcase. Everybody could see that the one crystal vase had cost her thirty guilders and that another, a little bigger, had cost her thirty-two fifty.

From that day on, she carried the nickname "Aunt Pessie-with-the-Pricetag."

The whole world of our neighbourhood was naturally in a state of suspense about what Aunt Breinie was going to do. She did not do anything but she got something, what she did was to get a loop in her intestine! In those days a loop in the intestine was called a knot, and it was a life-and-death matter, but mostly death.

You can see immediately what kind of good-luck birds rich people sometimes are. When Aunt Breinie was stretched out there in the hospital, the professor discovered that it wasn't really a knot in the intestine but what is nowadays called appendicitis. She turned out to be one of the first who had her appendix operated on, and I don't have to tell you how she talked about it when she finally got well and was back home again. Just as other rich people boast about their jewels, so she bragged about her appendix, which they had taken away from her, and they knocked her out with a pincher on her nose so that she didn't feel anything of the operation and she only blabbed to her Sjaje what she first said when she came out from under the ether. This was because the operating nurse had told her that there was a man before her who was operated on and when he was coming to, the first thing he said was, "Sari, move over with your big fat *tochis*."

Aunt Pessie-with-the Pricetag just went to pieces from jealousy. For, no matter how much money you have, where can you go out and buy an appendicitis operation? Nowhere of course. So everybody thought that Pessie had lost the war against Aunt Breinie, but then something very mysterious happened to Aunt Pessie-with-the-Pricetag.

For three whole weeks Pessie did not come out in the street. She sat at home, and she did not receive anybody. When the three weeks were over, out she came triumphantly… Take one guess, what did she come out with?

With a set of false teeth!

In those days that was also a great rarity, and you understand how the family stared when one evening she suddenly took her upper and lower plates out of her mouth and let everybody look at them.

Like a house afire the news swept through the neighbourhood on burning tongues of gossip. Aunt Pessie-with-the-Pricetag has bought herself some false teeth, they were saying. From Dentist Klinger on the Frederiksplein. They had cost her at least a thousand guilders. Unbelievable …

You will be asking what all these things had to do with me, Zelik, the unlucky nephew. And how did I miss out on the two inheritances? That I shall now relate, so pay attention.

At the time I am talking about, I was just twelve years old, give or take a few months. I was what you say, not *meshuga*. Someone said once, If you yell 'smart aleck' Zelik turns his head." In those days that was a compliment for a boy not yet *Bar Mitzvah*.

Well, one evening the whole mishpocheh was sitting around our house. Aunt Pessie-with-the-Pricetag was there too, and you could feel that she was dying to talk about her false teeth. But nobody gave her the chance because they were talking about something else all the time. And then all of a sudden, when it got quiet, I piped up, "Auntie, let us have a look at your plates, how about it? Just take them out of your mouth."

Naturally, she didn't hesitate, and all the rest of the evening everybody had to hear how Dentist Klinger first pulled all her molars and incisors, painlessly, but she didn't have to be put to sleep; and how he then took her mouth measurements, because she could have a ready-made set or get a set made to order. When Aunt Pessie finally went home that night, what did she do but put ten cents in my hand. From that evening on, I always took the trouble to be around when Aunt Breinie or Aunt Pessie-with-the-Pricetag was coming for a visit.

To give Aunt Breinie the same pleasure, I would ask if she would tell about her operation. Then I got ten cents from her, just like the other aunt gave me money if I brought her teeth into the conversation.

Only when they came visiting together did things get a little complicated. I wanted to hold onto both of them as clients, and they were always competing. It left me in the middle. Neither one of the aunts had children, and in the family it was soon being said, "This Zelik is a real lucky dog. Just listen to what I am predicting. If Aunt Breinie or Aunt Pessie-with-the-Pricetag—G-d keep us and save us— shut their eyes for good, then Zelik is getting the money… from both of them."

Because of all that talk I got pretty high-nosed. I became cocky, until one evening I had brought the conversation around again to the false teeth, but did not get any ten cents in return. I became so angry that I planned for myself a revenge and the opportunity for that revenge came very quickly.

It was an evening when both aunts were paying a call on my mother. During a lull in the conversation I said:

"Aunt Pessie, let us see your false teeth just once more."
For appearance sake, she resisted, "Ach, silly boy, I have let
you see them so often." Then I was supposed to beg again
that I still would like to see the teeth. That's how the game
was supposed to work. But instead of that, I said, "Well,
don't let me see them, then. I should worry. I don't think
those teeth are so much, anyway. But you ought to see
Aunt Breinie's appendicitis. She let me see where she got
operated on, and it's a beautiful sight."

The consequence of this was completely unexpected.
From my mother I got a whack which I can still feel, even
though it was way back when I was only twelve years old.
Aunt Breinie began to screech and threw herself into a
nervous fit from shame. And Aunt Pessie-with-the-Pricetag
walked out of the door and stayed away for two years from
sheer anger.

That's how I spoiled my chance for two jeroushos
together worth a million—oh, was I just saying a hundred
thousand—anyway, that's a pretty good amount, too, as
inheritances go.

AT THE OPERA

On Saturday night the people from the Jewish district visit other parts of town.

A week of hard work has ended, the day of rest has been enjoyed, now it is time for the evening out. They stroll to Carré, the opera-house, and squeeze together in the upper gallery. Let the rich folks down below flaunt themselves in their expensive seats. Those who have come for art solely, enjoy two song festivals for half price.

First there is the official song festival, the one on the stage. The second, unofficial one takes place during the intermission. Nobody in the upper tiers goes to the coffee-room, intermission or not, their song festival continues all the same. They break into arias with long drawn-out resonant tones.

Their relatives will say of them later "He has sung in Carré…" and then add sarcastically …" during the Intermission."

The connoisseurs in their cheap seats listen to them with affection and critical attention. Rendering and diction are a matter of secondary importance to them, they do not care whether the chanted text tallies with the official libretto. For them only the melody and the vocal power counts.

One connoisseur says to another "That young man over there has a beautiful voice. What a *kol*!"

"Oy, no wonder, don't you know who his grandfather was?"

"How should I know? I do not know that young fellow at all."

"Kerpel…Kerpel! His grandfather was Kerpel, the greatest singer the world has ever known. What are you telling me now, you've never heard of Kerpel? You should be ashamed. You talk of opera and you've never heard of Kerpel?"

Says the other "If you ask me, his voice reminds me a little of Isalberti."

"Isalberti? Isalberti? That's the last straw! Honest to G-d, I am surprised that you're not telling me his voice sounds like that of Else Grassau. That voice… There is only one voice that boy reminds me of… You don't know whom I'm referring to? Well, all right, I'll tell you. The voice of Jacques Urlus. Yes sir, no other than Jacques Urlus."

"Now that you mention that name… Yes, you're right, Jacques Urlus. No other. Like two drops of water Urlus. But it has a touch of Orelio in it too."

The voluntary arias that arise from the gallery are unannounced, they bubble up from a feeling of overflowing musicality. The spontaneous singer represents the voice of the audience. When they give voice to the popular arias, the gallery turns into a secularised synagogue with the voluntary soloist as the cantor.

The congregation sings the opening theme of Leoncavallo's opera *I paggliacci*.

CANTOR: "Yes. We are people too…"
CONGREGATION: "Of flesh and blood…

Perhaps it is due to the fact that the composer was a Jew, or to the exceptional harmony of his music, or perhaps to the contents of the opera, but no fragment is so much in demand as the opening theme of

The Huguenots by Meyerbeer.

CANTOR: "Parisians, leave your homes…"
CONGREGATION: "Ding, dong."
CANTOR: "Dim the lights, don't make a sound."
CONGREGATION: "Ding dong."
CANTOR: "Let the bells ring, bells of the evening hour…"

Notwithstanding the enormous amount of space within Carré, and its many seats, one opera house is not enough for the Jews of Amsterdam. Filled with a raving hunger for the fine arts, they also stream to the Playhouse in French Lane. Visitors to that theatre are let into the auditorium after having to wander for forty years through a lobby as vast as a desert, where icy winds supply double pneumonia's at half price. The hall itself has a stale smell and between the rows of seats a large stove is burning. The carpets on the floor consist of cheap matting and the chairs are rickety. In that sweltering barn, however, true art is presented.

Henri de Lagardière ("He's not dead, he is alive!")...
Lazaro the Herdsman ("My Father a Murderer?")...
Rose Kate ("or the Tragedy of the Blacksmith"). In this
immortal genre, "The Two Orphans" form the culmination
point. One night a couple of teenage girls are watching the
"Two Orphans". On the stage the two orphan girls drift on
waves of syrup, from misfortune to calamity. The teenagers
are giggling at this sentimental sugar cake, but in the row in
front of them, a woman is sobbing as if she has just heard
for the first time of the destruction of the Temple. Annoyed
by the giggles of the girls, she turns around and reproaches
them with tears in her eyes, "How can you spoil my
evening so?"

The theatre in French Lane also presents a never ending
series of Emil Zola's play "The Pub." The Jewish audience
never seems to get enough of the delirium scene. Perhaps
this is so because they never drink a drop of alcohol themselves, they prefer pickled herring. After the play, when they
leave the theatre they re-enact the scene. "Rats...
Rats...Rats. I see nothing but rats..."

At this point there's always some funny relative who
advises, "Then take a cat!"

The Tip Top theatre is in Jewish Breestreet. The people so
love this theatre, that they call it "Tsip Tsop". That is how
one calls a beloved child, not by its official name but by a
word that mispronounces it in child-talk. Tsip Tsop, blessed
may it be, omein-we-omein.

Others contemptuously call it the peanut theatre
because shiploads of peanuts are devoured there daily. After
each performance, cleaning women have to shovel tons of

empty shells from the floor, even though a notice at the entrance of the Tsip Tsop says "One is kindly requested to bring along only *shelled* peanuts."

The Director of the theatre, Uncle Joseph, has an infallible instinct for knowing exactly what his public wants to see. When "Talkies", talking films, were first introduced in Holland, he turned his theatre into a cinema. But not just an ordinary cinema. No, into a synagogue. A Cine-gogue!

The stage curtain he replaced with two beautifully painted folding doors. Behind them, in front of the screen, was the pianist and the choir whose task it was to put the audience in the right mood with fine songs like Kol Nidrei and the melodies of Chanukkah.

One of the first films shown in the Tsip Tsop was Sunny Boy, starring Al Jolson. The loudspeakers had trouble in reproducing certain sounds, so Al appeared to have a speech-defect in pronouncing the letters "s" and "f". Nevertheless, the film got a roaring reception, because the predominantly Jewish audience was aware that Jolson was one of them, and appreciated that the film-script was not exactly anti-Semitic either.

About the Tsip Tsop many funny tales are told. The theatre had five doors at the side which opened up into an alley, and which served as emergency exits. These doors were not exactly sound-proof and the alley was rather noisy. On the sidewalk outside, push carts and barrows with goods were standing in a long, continuous row. The vendors leaned against the doors of the Tsip Tsop loudly praising their wares. Meanwhile, inside the theatre, Van Briene, the explicator, walked up and down the tiers of seats trying to get himself heard. Not all new films were supplied with a sound track, and when a silent movie was shown, Van Briene had to fill in the dialogue accompanied by the man at the piano. The vendors outside the theatre, with their loud voices, kept interrupting him so he always tried to finish his lines quickly within the breathing space which even a hawker of pears cannot do without. Usually he succeeded in this, but occasionally he did not, and then funny situations arose.

Someone tells, "Yesterday afternoon I was in the Tsip Tsop. Van Briene walks through the theatre and chants, 'The count takes the maiden in his arms. He murmurs 'My love, at last we are alone'."

At the same moment from the outside we hear "Fine untouched pears, sweet virginal pears!"

Further on in the film, Van Briene keeps silent because the scene in the film is so touching. The piano player does not make a sound and the audience is silent too. On the screen, the Count gives the Countess a mushy kiss. At that precise instant, someone outside calls out "How lovely they are, so juicy'!"

The fellow who told that story may have been joking but it certainly is not a joke that one night a woman, a regular customer, came to the theatre and told Hes, the doorman "Tomorrow I have to go to the hospital to have a dangerous operation. I told my David 'You know what I'll do? Tonight I will go to the Tsip Tsop for a while, so at least I will not have missed that show'."

When there is unemployment in the diamond industry, polishers who are out of work sometimes spend an afternoon at the Tsip Tsop to pass away the time. However, on one such afternoon an urgent message can be delivered at their home from someone from the factory. "Lady, they want your husband to come directly because the boss has some work for him."

Ma hurries to the Tsip Tsop. She tells Hes "I have to see my husband at once. He can get work."

She is let in and Hes walks with a torch in his hand along the rows of seats. The woman walks alongside him, right until she has found her husband. Nobody in the audience objects. On the contrary, where in the whole world will you find a theatre that so takes into account the daily cares of its customers? Of course, this can lead to awkward situations. For instance, when a woman, accompanied by Hes goes looking for her husband and finds him holding hands in the dark with the neighbour's wife.

Highlights in the life of the Tsip Tsop are the films with a Jewish topic. They make a deep impression and people talk about them for years. *Dybuk*, the Polish-Jewish film, *Yidd'l mit de Fidd'l*, and the film which Uncle Joseph had made specially for showing at the Tsip Tsop theatre, the film *Simche and Tsuris*, Joy and Sorrow…

GENERAL EISENHOWER CALLED HIM 'THE GREATEST LIVING EXPERT ON SECURITY'

ORESTE PINTO WAS A TYPICAL SEPHARDIC type with dark curly hair. He was a nervous, clever boy with pale eyes. He and a young friend of his called Appie enjoyed a notorious reputation in the Jewish quarter.

People called the pair 'the two comedians' because they were always full of practical jokes. They carried out an act and divided their role-playing. Appie usually was the one who invented the practical joke, and then it was Oreste who talked somebody into being the victim. Even as a youngster, he already demonstrated that capacity which would later prove to be his fame. By instinct Oreste knew precisely the weak spots in the psychological armour of the people he met, and with complete self-assurance he always directed his attack on that weak spot.

I will give you an example of the way they went about. For instance, Appie proposed that they sell the idea to some house-wife that they had devised a way to yank the table-cloth from under the plates and dishes on her dining table without disturbing them.

The only question was, who would be willing to accept a demonstration? That's where Oreste's skill came in. Unhesitatingly he would approach Mrs. So-and-so. When the two boys were inside the house, he did the talking. Not nagging or childish, but suggestive, one might even say hypnotic.

It was strange, but somehow he always achieved what he wanted. A lot of plates and saucers were broken to smithereens in the houses they visited. Yet not one of the housewives refused a trial, they just couldn't. It was very strange for a twelve-year-old boy to possess such a compelling power over adults.

Later, when he was in his fifties, I asked Oreste whether he had an explanation for the strange power he could exercise over people.

"No…not an explanation," he answered. "The only thing I know is that I have always been terribly scared. I can't recall a day in my life when I didn't wake up with a feeling of fear. My greatest fear was that my friends would find out that I was a coward. That they would discover how yellow I was inside drove me to madly daring deeds that gave me superhuman powers. Do you understand what I am trying to say?"

"Yes and no," I admitted. "That so-called magician's trick with the tablecloth and china for instance, what on earth has that to do with your fear?"

"You don't know the full story yet," he said seriously. "It always started like this: My friend Appie told me that he had conceived some idea, the tablecloth trick, for instance. And then he asked me, "Oreste, are you scared to ask people to do it?"

He was daring me to do it and I saw the importance of his dare magnified a thousand times. So it was I who went to those people in the end and made the pitch. But in fact it wasn't really me who hypnotised those victims, it was the other way around… I was the one who was hypnotised, because I was obsessed by the fear that they would see through my cowardice.

"Have you ever played with a loaded gun?" he asked me then. "Have you ever felt the tingling sensation that you have to put that weapon against your head and pull the trigger? You haven't? Well, I have. It is a sensation gruesome and voluptuously seductive at the same time. It's like dancing on the edge of a cliff, it's hypnotising. And then the triumph when you can put that cold thing down and know that you are stronger than that killing machine.

Oreste Pinto also exercised a strange effect on animals. I myself have witnessed the weird attraction he had for them. During the war, when we were both in England, he used to visit our house in Stoke Poges, west of London. I don't know of a more appropriate word than "creepy" to describe the emotions of myself and my family when Oreste "talked with the cat."

Most normal people caress a cat and whisper something in it's ear. But not he. When he opened the gate to enter our garden, pussy jumped out of the house. The creature just ran to meet him. From its mouth came a constant current of uncommon sounds. Somehow you got the impression that the dumb animal wanted to report everything that had happened since our guest had been with us last. Then Oreste squatted and "talked back" (I cannot find a better description) in non-human sounds.

We lived in the countryside and raised chickens at the time. Quite a flock was running about in our back yard. One of the fowls, a hen, seemed to be especially fond of Oreste. In fact, judging by the emotional way she behaved, that chicken seemed to be head-over-heels in love with him. He called her Sarah.

Now, in my opinion, chickens are the silliest animals that ever roamed the earth, fit only to lay eggs and to be cooked in the end. Sarah was by no means an exception. But you should have seen that hen whenever Oreste came to visit us. She ran to the wire fence to get as close to him as possible. And then she started talking, yes talking. Very excited cackling, all sorts of fowl-nonsense, and without interruption. Oreste squatted on his haunches near her at the fence and talked back to her. With low organ-tones in his throat and now and then a high pitch.

Oreste had a flat in London. He told me one day that in the London Zoo there was a chimpanzee that he had caught years ago, before the war, when he hunted in Africa. He asked me whether I would like to meet his friend.

"Friend" that's how he put it.

In retrospect, I consider this visit to the Zoo one of the strangest adventures of my entire life, and I daresay that being a roving reporter I have seen quite a number of weird things. From the moment Oreste passed through the big gate, it seemed as if all the animals had received some stimulating injection. They became very lively in their cages and I got the mad feeling that if there had been no bars on those cages, all of them would have lined up for us like a guard of honour.

The mountain sheep with their grey smelly beards went

out of their minds. Up they reared, pressed against the gate,
heads up, sticking their pointed beards up in the air.
Present arms!

The chimpanzee behaved like an old friend should. She
made funny noises and performed all sorts of acrobatics,
showing off as if to say, "Look at all the things I've
learned."

Later, when we had a cup of tea together, Oreste asked
me what I thought of the chimp. My voice sounded hoarse
when I replied "In the Middle Ages they would have
accused you of being possessed by the devil. You would
have been burned at the stake for witchcraft."

"Maybe I have been burned at the stake," Oreste retort-
ed in perfect seriousness.

"Don't be silly," I said. "Now please give me an honest
explanation."

"I'm convinced that it is just a matter of smell, "he said
pensively. "If someone is really fond of animals, he smells
different to them."

When he was a young man, living with his parents on
Weesperzijde Street in Amsterdam, Oreste had little money.
He started to do some trading on the side and then he
decided he would earn his living by being a boxer. He did
quite well in that profession as a lightweight or something,
and one day, when he had a boxing match in Paris, a
stranger visited him in his dressing room. The stranger told
him he was a police inspector. Would Oreste Pinto be willing to accept a well-paid job in France? Be the personal
bodyguard of Monsieur the High-Up? That bigwig was
afraid that someday, someone would take a pot shot at him.

It was a rather comical situation, Oreste, the self-admitted personification of fear, was asked to become a bodyguard to a man who was riddled with fear, as well.

But he took the job and thus it came about that he landed in the international underworld because his boss turned out to be the Big Johnnie of French counter-espionage.

When World War I broke out Oreste was in Paris and the French wanted somebody who was willing to move to Berlin to look around and report back to them once in a while. Big Johnnie asked Oreste what he thought about it. If he had asked, "Will you go to Berlin to do some spying for us," Oreste might have refused. But Big Johnnie knew his bodyguard well by now, so he asked him, "Would you dare to live in Berlin?"

Oreste could not say "no" when it was put that way to him.

He had a clever way to get his reports through the lines to Paris. The French had suggested all sorts of traditional tricks—invisible ink and that sort of thing, but he had a much better idea. In Holland he had a lady friend who was in love with him and who would be glad to share his bed in Berlin. But first, he said, she would have to go through a course in lace-making. That's right…making lace. The French thought that Oreste had gone completely out of his mind when he told them this, but after he'd explained his scheme, they hailed him as a genius. His idea was very simple. They cooked up an intricate code for him with ornaments, arabesques, and frills. The lady friend learned how to translate the code into beautiful lace work.

So a Dutchman whose passport said that he was born of

German parents arrived in Berlin around March 1915. Herr Heinz Müller was his name and together with his wife "Frau Müller" he led a peaceful and quiet life in the Kaiser's capital. Once every three months Frau Müller went to Holland to visit her relatives. She did not carry much luggage and she wore a rather cheap-looking, home-made lace petticoat…

This went well for about a year but then the German counter-espionage somehow became suspicious of this Müller couple. By sheer luck, Frau Müller happened to be in Holland at the time, so she was in no danger. Oreste discovered that the police were looking for him while staying in Berlin, and tried to escape to Holland. He jumped from a moving train near the German–Dutch frontier, because he had a hunch that they would wait to arrest him at the next station.

He intended to get across the rest of the distance on foot because, at that point, it was only a couple of miles to the border. But when he was halfway, he saw twelve men approaching in a half-circle, each man about a thirty yard distance from the other. The Huns were after him! The visibility was good and Oreste himself was near one outer end of the half-circle.

When he recounted his adventure to me thirty years later, he confessed that this was the supreme moment of fear in his life. "But I realised that I had to control myself, and at once the panic disappeared. How can I explain it to you? I felt as if I had split into two, one part of me was scared stiff and the other walked and heard and looked and moved as a perfectly normal being.

"I crouched close to the ground til the line of men was

about even with me. Then, as the fellow closest to me looked the other way, I stood up, shouted something in German, and pointed in front of me. I did not have to try to create any impression that I belonged to the hunting party. No, I was positively sure that I actually *was* one of them. And the craziest thing was that they did not doubt for one single moment that I was one of them. The hunt went on for an hour or so, and then they shouted that the "verdammte spitzel" (dammed spy) could not be found and that we had to report back. I remained in the rear, dropped out of the group, and later found my way safely to the frontier."

Oreste returned to Paris. The officials there were highly satisfied with his work but for obvious reasons he could not be sent to Berlin again. The French decided to use him somewhere else. By that time the armies had dug themselves deep in the trenches of Northern France. These lines were infested with spies, both men and women, who were used mostly for reconnaissance and intelligence about troop movements and information about the morale of the troops. Small fry, these junior grade spies were, but nasty as hornets. Was Oreste willing to bear the responsibility for counter-espionage in a particular sector of the line?

Before Oreste could answer, his chief told him, "Quite a lot of fellows who were offered this assignment refused because of the great danger involved. If they chance to catch you, they'll shoot you on the spot.

At being offered that dare, Oreste couldn't say no.

Later, he used to call this period in Northern France the lousiest time of his life. He didn't really want to talk about what happened. The only thing he told me was, that in all he sent about forty men and women to the firing squad.

After World War I, Oreste said goodbye to the French and returned to Amsterdam. It was August 31, 1919, Queen Wilhelmina's birthday. And what a birthday it was. The first carefree day of national rejoicing after four years of continuous fears of invasion and scarcity of food. The streets of Amsterdam were a heaving sea of dancing, singing crowds.

Oreste strolled along and felt very happy but suddenly he became embroiled in a street fight. Some drunken sailors tried to get two women to join them in the street dancing. The women refused, and the sailors insisted and got angry. The women started shrieking...Oreste attacked, knocked one sailor unconscious, gave the second a kick in the shins, sent the third sprawling in the gutter, the fourth running away. The whole fight lasted no longer than a few minutes.

The two women thanked him profusely. They turned out to be British. Oreste did not say no when they asked him to see them safely to their hotel.

The next day, they invited him for lunch and he asked them whether they would like him to show them Amsterdam. Well, one thing led to another...Eventually, Oreste married one of them and the couple moved to a nice house in Blackpool.

I do not know what Oreste Pinto did between the two world wars. The only thing I know is that his marriage flopped and that he moved from Blackpool to London.

When, in 1933, the Nazis assumed power in Germany, he was asked by the British to assume his old job of counter-espionage. His special job was educating people who were to smoke out spies. The training programme went something like this:

Oreste pretended to be a spy caught by the service and his pupils had to try to unmask him. In doing so, they had to pay special attention to secret methods of passing information. During the period he worked for the British, it was suggested to him that he should apply for naturalisation. He could become a British subject if he wanted to. But he said no.

"Why did you refuse?" I asked him once.

"Because Holland is my Mother Country," he replied.

I remember that at the time I considered this expression "Mother Country" rather strange. We talked to each other in Dutch of course, and in that language we say "Vaderland", which means "Fatherland". I thought that his "Moederland" (Motherland) must be a slip of the tongue.

When World War II finally broke out, Oreste happened to still be in England. He was eager to play his part in the big show because he hated the Nazis like the plague. He hunted everyone down against whom the slightest suspicion existed and carried out this job with a zeal and energy that surpassed by far a normal sense of duty, even in spy-hunting. And he practically never failed.

If Oreste Pinto said "I don't like the looks of that chap," you could count on it that sooner or later he would get his man and unmask him as a spy. This was demonstrated in a remarkable way in the case of Jan Gerrit Bronkema.

I heard that name for the first time when I met Oreste

in my London club. We had lunch together there, and he asked me if I ever heard of anyone named Jan Gerrit Bronkema who was supposed to come from a village near Utrecht.

"No…the name doesn't ring a bell," I had to admit.

"Are you quite sure? Never heard of a Dutch quisling by that name?"

"Never. But listen, there are some people here in London who come from near Utrecht. Perhaps they know something about him."

"Oh, that's not the problem, the chap comes from that village all right. He isn't lying about that. But he arrived here two months ago and from the first moment I heard his name, I had this funny feeling about him."

"What do you mean?"

Oreste then told me what he knew about this Jan Gerrit Brinkema.

When Dutch people escaped from Nazi-occupied Holland and made their way to Great Britain, they were brought to an old school building in the country. There they were questioned by tough and skilled counter-espionage officers in order to determine whether they were courageous Dutch patriots, or spies, sent by the Germans. Jan Gerrit Bronkema had arrived in a small sailing boat, together with six other men. After all seven had been questioned, the intelligence officers reported that nothing suspicious had caught their attention. None of them looked happier than this Jan Gerrit, the interrogators reported. That Bronkema sang patriotic songs all day. After he had spent two months in the old school building (interrogations usually lasted as long as that) he was still singing the Dutch national anthem and other songs of that kind.

"That's not normal," Oreste told me. "When I read that in the reports, I knew that man was pretending. Love for one's country is a splendid thing, of course, but singing the "Wilhelmus" (the Dutch national anthem) twenty-four hours a day and keeping it up for two months, means that this fellow wants to hide something from us."

From the moment that he had read the report, there wasn't a doubt in Oreste's mind that Jan Gerrit Bronkema was a spy masquerading as a fugitive from Naziism.

"I knew for certain that this blighter was no good. I admit that I started my investigation with a strong prejudice, but that's the way I work," he explained to me. "In cases such as this, I start with the conclusion, as if someone whispers it into my ear. Then I go to work in order to prove that I was right in the first place. I start by accusing the suspect, and when they deny my charges I turn on the screws. In the end they always confess—always. I have never failed. And once that spy pleads guilty, *I send him back to his mother.*"

Oreste always used that peculiar phrase when he wanted to say that he had sent someone to the gallows. He had "*Sent him back to his mother…*" I had never heard this expression with such a cruel connotation used before.

From the moment his intuition had told him that Jan Gerrit Bronkema was a spy, Oreste followed his trail like a bloodhound. He read and reread all reports about Bronkema until he knew all the facts about him by heart. However, he didn't mention his suspicions to his superiors yet, because in fact there was no shadow of evidence against Bronkema except that he bored everybody within hearing to death with his patriotic songs.

After our conversation in my club, Oreste kept me informed about further developments in the case. Bronkema had been released from the old school building in the country because he was considered safe. He rented a flat near Paddington Station in London, got a small job and lived very quietly. At 9 a.m. on the dot he was at his desk. He never entered a pub or visited a cinema. He didn't appear to have friends and never had any visitors. A decent, quiet man, he seemed. "Too quiet for me," commented Oreste. "Such people simply don't exist."

But even after Bronkema had been in England for four whole months, there was still no proof that he wasn't what he pretended to be.

"If I were you," I told Oreste, "I would admit that I was wrong."

"I know for certain he's a spy," Oreste shouted angrily.

I grinned. "All right," I said, "then arrest him! But if you've made a mistake you will be in deep trouble. He'll sure raise hell."

"Are you telling me that I haven't the guts to have him arrested?" asked Oreste and had Bronkema thrown into jail that same afternoon.

The next day he phoned to tell me about what happened next. "I've interrogated him for four hours this morning ," he reported. "He denies everything, of course. He continues to say that he's a true patriot. Claims that he is the defender of the House of Orange. Says that he is renowned in the province of Utrecht for his heroic deeds against the Nazis. At one point he cried, 'Mr Pinto, if my old father who is in heaven, knew that you suspected me of being a spy for those criminals, he would turn in his grave.' That, and a lot more of such trash. I let him go home in the end. He's just left my office."

"So you are giving up?"

"No," Oreste said abruptly. "I don't intend to do so at all. That Bronkema is a spy, there's still no doubt in my mind about it. This afternoon I'll have someone looking around his flat, and when he comes home from work I'll have him picked up again. I am sure he hid something there, he was scared stiff."

"What will you say to him then?" I asked.

"First I am going to present him with a detailed description of an execution by hanging. Did you ever witness such an execution, Meyer? I have, several times. I am in the habit of accompanying my customers during their last stroll to the gallows so that I can personally deliver them back to their mother."

Back to their mother!

"And from each of them I keep a souvenir. I have a cigarette case from one of them and a little mirror from another spy whom I caught. I am really fond of my little souvenirs, and so I'll tell Jan Gerrit Bronkema. I'll show him the cigarette case and the mirror and all my other little remembrances. Then I'll tell him how I hunted down these spies, how they looked when they confessed, how they spent their last hour in their cell. And I will tell him that I will stand in the corridor when he passes on his way to his mother as well."

That night, Oreste phoned me again. "I know enough" he told me. "When I started questioning him again this afternoon he first acted very brazenly, but when I showed him my souvenirs he got shaky. So I went on. Finally. I gave

him a detailed description of the emotions a man feels
when he mounts the platform of the gallows and the
hangman puts a rope around his neck. What he feels when
the support under his feet is drawn away and the noose
gets tighter around his neck until, against his will, he has to
stick out his tongue. Then in his neck he feels a shock, just
a little shock, and everything gets red and he hears the
thunder of an ocean far in the distance and then he has
returned to his mother. I described all that to Bronkema
with full details."

"How did he react," I asked, somewhat shaken.

Oreste laughed. "He grew as pale as a bed sheet. He
looked at the window, and in his eyes I read, 'I'll jump,
then this Pinto cannot torture me any longer.'

So I did not let him go home, tonight he'll sleep in a
cell. In the meantime, I'm going to read the Bible."

"The Bible?" I asked surprised.

"Yes. When we searched his house we found a Bible
hidden behind the bread basket. Now, who would ever
hide a Bible behind a bread basket? So tonight I will read
both the Old and New Testament in it very carefully."

Next morning Oreste was waiting for me in my office.
He beamed and he started talking immediately. "Bronkema
has confessed," he told me. "This morning at seven. He has
spilled everything he knew..."

I was flabbergasted.

Oreste said smilingly "I told you, I told you from the
start that he was no good. But you were quite right, I did-
n't have any proof. If he had not hidden that Bible behind
the bread basket, he might still be a free man. I read that
book very carefully. Page after page, I studied with a mag-

nifying glass. And then I found a small pinpoint hole in Samuel I. It took me the whole night to find the other holes, but at half past six, I had all the parts. They formed an address in Stockholm."

I looked at my friend with open admiration. He pretended not to notice and went on. "I did not waste any words this morning. I entered his cell saying, 'Good morning.' He said 'Good morning' too. Then I said 'Best regards from Svensson in Stockholm.'

He collapsed immediately, confessed everything. Of course, I had already broken him. He was supposed to gather information about the demolition in London after the Nazi bombardments. They told him to write his reports in invisible ink in the margin of innocent letters to a so-called friend in Stockholm. It might never have been detected."

"And how is he now?"

"Calm. Pretty calm. He gave me a hand and said that I had to do my duty, just as he had to do his. And he told me that from the very first moment he saw me, he saw that I had his death in my eyes. The funny thing is that he'd seen me even before I interrogated him. Apparently, three months ago some of my colleagues had taken him to the canteen for lunch when they were questioning him, and that's where he saw me sitting at a table. He says he didn't know who I was, but that I looked his way—well the way one sometimes looks at people without really seeing them. And yet at that moment, he says, he was certain that I would send him to the gallows. Strange, isn't it? Do you think it has something to do with me having been burned at the stake in the Middle Ages?"

When the Allied armies led by General Eisenhower invaded the European continent, Oreste Pinto got a special assignment. He had to interrogate important prisoners of war. As it happened, he got practically only Nazi S.S. officers. I was a war correspondent with the Allied forces and heard the most fantastic stories about how he used to "break" these Nazi toughs. Some he approached in "Prussian" fashion, with shouting and fist-banging on the table. Other prisoners he scared stiff by subtle suggestions. One of his most successful tricks was to pretend that he was a Russian officer who had come to take the SS-er to the Soviet Union. Then he came strutting in pretending that he was that Russian, filled to the eyebrows with hatred because of the atrocities the S.S. had carried out in his homeland. He showed the photographs of homes in Kharkov burned down, men hanging from trees, and then with a tear-choked voice begged them to allow him to take the prisoner to Kharkov in order to have him tried there. "We Russians are hard, you British and Americans are softies," he would say. So I want to take this man to be tried by my own people…"

Oreste never got that S.S. man, because as soon as he had left the room, the Nazi hastily told the Americans or British all he knew and hadn't wanted to tell Oreste.

"Yesterday, I sent another back to his mother, " Oreste would announce in the officer's mess.

After Germany was defeated, he got out of the army. Years later, I met him on Damrak street in Amsterdam. He looked pale. His hair had turned to grey and his eyes were dead. A cadaverous man, walking in bright sunlight. He told me that he had been decorated for his spy catching work by General Eisenhower himself, who had called him "the greatest living expert on security."

"It's nice to be called that," he told me "but I'd rather be a healthy man again. I am stiff from arthritis. A couple of months ago some military quack gave me the shock of my life. He told me that I had cancer and that I had only three more months to live. So I flew to London to have X-rays taken. What terrible fear I had that in three months' time I was going to die. I had sent so many people to the gallows and now I was afraid to die myself, ha, ha, ha. But it turned out not to be cancer...ha, ha, ha, only arthritis, neglected arthritis. What a joke. I'm convinced that so-called doctor who told me I had cancer was fooling me on purpose. He got what he wanted, he scared me to death. I suppose he told my colleagues and they all had a big laugh together. They must have seen how frightened I was." Oreste laughed hoarsely. "I could kill them, all of them," he said. "I didn't want to see any of them anymore after that ordeal, so I resigned from the service. I'm going back to my flat in London and I'll spend the rest of my days there with my souvenirs, the cigarette cases, guns, diaries, mirrors, and pocket combs, all the things which remind me of the people I sent back to their mothers.

And at night I'll play phonograph records. You know my favourite?"

Did I know his favourite? Of course I did! Oreste was so fond of that record that he brought it with him every time he visited our house for a weekend, all through those war days in England. It seemed that he could not live without that music. It was the record on which Sophie Tucker sings of her Jewish mother, "My Yiddische Mama".

The first part of that record is a sort of dialogue. Oreste
used to listen intently. When Sophie Tucker relates that her
mother always had a child to breastfeed ("Und immer ein
kind gewickelt") tears would come streaming down his
cheeks. He'd play that sentimental record three or four
times in a row, and he'd cry as if his heart would break…

No, I will not venture to bring Freud and Jung and the
other psychiatrists into it, but sometime, somewhere in the
psychological clockwork of this strange man, something
must have gone wrong. Something perhaps caused by an
event, a word, an incident—G-d knows what—in that
family on Weesperzijde Street in Amsterdam. Something
that had to do with his mother…

BACKGROUNDS

Long ago they were driven from the land where they were one people, and where they received the law which they passed on to the world. Their "Ten Commandments" are still the backbone of what we call Western civilisation. Within the confines of their persecution they guarded the memory of Eretz, the land of Israel so dearly, that through the ages they wandered carrying that land with them. For two thousand years they carried it on their shoulders and that is why so many Jews have a slightly bent back.

Scattered over the wide world, they still remained one nation. Desert sands buried in thick layers the cities where they had once dwelt, and the cities of their enemies. The language of the Babylonians withered, but the Jews kept the speech of Miriam, David and Solomon living like fresh water. Again and again the sons of Haman stood up to exterminate them, and always in the final reckoning the persecuted stood at the gallows where their tyrants were hanged.

Goods, possessions and wealth are not really important, when things are at their blackest, only staying alive is. If even that is no longer possible, the lives of the children must be saved. Therefore, the aim of all their toil is the well-being of their children. They must leave behind a world for their off-spring which will be better than the one in which they themselves were born. Deep in their hearts they regard worldly goods of less value than the bond which joins all Jews together, so they can quarrel with each other fiercely, knowing all the time that in the end they will make up again.

And then, of course, they share a certain type of sad humour.

When two Jews meet, in nine out of ten cases they tell each other funny stories about two men who meet each other and start a conversation.

"Do you know this joke? Two Jews meet each other…"

Says the other "Oah…Again a joke of two Jews who meet each other. Don't you know anything else?"

Says the first one "Sure. You listen. Two China-men meet each other. Says the one China-man to the other China-man 'Do you already have matzoth in the house for Pesach?'"

The sky above the old district in Amsterdam is saturated with such stories. A man suddenly realises that the elusive joke that has floated above the heads of everybody, has condensed in his brain. Then, in no time at all, it speeds from mouth to mouth.

Many of the stories are about immigrants from Eastern Europe. The Jews of Amsterdam know deep in their hearts that these wanderers are what they themselves always fear to become. So if in their jokes they make fun of the Jews who have recently arrived from Russia and Poland, they really poke fun at themselves.

Here's an example of such a story.

On board an ocean steamer on the way to America, one Polish Jew wakes up another in the middle of the night.

"Wake up, wake up, the ship is sinking!"

Says the other sleepily "Do you have to wake me up for that? Is it *my* ship?"

And then this one:

A man says to his neighbour "I hear that you have let yourself be baptised. That I do not understand. Your brother had himself baptised a year ago. Okay, that I understand, he always wanted to be assimilated. But you? Why have you decided to become a Christian?" Says the other "To tell you the truth, I did it for my brother. He did not have any Christian friends."

However, their life does not merely consist of uncertainties. Comparatively secure they feel themselves within their domestic circle. There is a firm bond between the members. They are also buttressed by the certainty that no Jew will let another down if things are at their worst.

A continuous appeal is made to those who are well off, and they give readily and liberally. Whatever you give to the poor, you will never lack yourself. He who helps his brother in distress finds grace in the eyes of G-d. They like to use the word *rachmones*, which means more than pity. It expresses being one with the sufferer, supporting him like you yourself would like to be helped when in need. Their compassion expresses itself in the interjection "Nebbish". He who says "nebbish" sincerely, can never have a heart of stone. He will even regard the most vicious criminal to be a *schlemiel*. Asked what the subtle difference is between a schlemiel and a nebbish, they will define the difference with a parable.

"A schlemiel is someone who lets everything drop from his hands, and a nebbish is someone who picks it all up for him."

Or they explain "A schlemiel is someone who falls on his back and breaks his nose."

Although the rich help readily, the next of kin, the *mishpocheh* must help first. That is a case of ethics. It would be a personal disgrace for each and every member of the family if strangers would say "Those poor souls have to go on the dole because their mishpocheh left them in a lurch."

But on the other hand, sometimes this can also lead to rows about money.

A man meets another on the street and says "How are things with you?"

Says the other "With me everything is fine."

Says the first one "How is that possible? Don't you have mishpocheh?

They have a mystical belief in the magic power of words and thoughts, so their everyday speech is full of formulas with which they hope to allay danger. Says a mother "My daughter has a good husband, *unbeschrien-unberufen*. Unbeschrien-unberufen is a magic charm to fend off evil spirits which may lay snares for the young woman whose mother announces so openly that she is a lucky person. That is because everywhere, Evil lies in wait to destroy Good. Says a young woman "My child is healthy and is growing up well."

Then the worried grandmother warns "Do not *beschrie* it."

They speak reluctantly of sickness and death. So, when they cannot avoid talking about death, for instance when they buy an insurance policy, they tone down what they fear by a funny paraphrase.

"Look Dad, now that you bought that insurance and if, G-d forbid, you close an eye after two hundred years, then at least Mother is provided for."

Says Father indignantly "Two hundred years? Three hundred years!"

Says someone to another, "You look bad…" The other one is ruffled and grumbles "I suppose that you did not see me on New Years Day, that only now you have come to bring me your good wishes."

But in a different context those same words can have a completely different meaning. When a woman comes home from her holidays, sunburnt and radiantly healthy, her friends tell her "Well, *you* look bad," which is meant as a compliment.

In this way a curious form of negative affirmation has snuck into their colloquy.

"Are you going for a walk?"

"No, I am taking the tram." This is said in a disgusted way.

By this they mean that they *are* going for a walk. It is just a matter of phrasing and accent.

A little old lady is standing on the corner of the street near the stopping-place of the tram. The tram grinds to a halt and the conductor enquires "Do you want to get on?"

The lady answers "No, I don't want to get on."

Then the conductor waits quietly until she has entered the tram safely. He knows the district and the people.

They have a boundless respect for superstitious acts and deeds. When a relative has died, they mourn eight days long, seated on a low stool or a cushion on the floor. So, woe betide the rash person who chances to put a cushion on the floor in order to sit on it in everyday life. Then they say of that act "One does not do a thing like that. That is a *niegish*."

Cause and effect are two sides of a coin to them. On days of mourning one puts a cushion on the floor, "therefore" putting a cushion on the floor can, G-d forbid… cause days of mourning.

At home, Father has his own chair. If someone else accidentally goes and sits on it, Father admonishes him gravely "At least wait until I'm dead. This is a niegish. "

That attitude also applies to clothing. "I never wear black ties because that is a niegish."

Or dishes:

"The day my sister died we had brown beans for supper, and do you know we also had brown beans when Mother closed her eyes? In my family we have a niegish regarding brown beans, we have never eaten them again since then."

Suddenly they can be tormented by anxious premonitions. Says someone, "I heard a fire-engine drive past and ran home like mad. I had such an awful feeling that it was our house that was on fire."

That is how these people were, when they still lived within the protective walls of a trusted setting. They always harboured premonitions of an impending doom. When that day finally came, when the Nazi gorillas dragged them from their houses and to their death, how many of them died not once, but many times?

YESTERDAY NEVER RETURNS

I HAD TWO AUNTS NAMED KATE, so our family called one of them Kate and the other one Duplikate.

Duplikate was a good soul, but when she was born, they had forgotten to sharpen her wits. In fact, she was as dumb as a doornail. Her absolute inability to understand even the simplest things was miraculous. For example, when we played Bingo and it was her turn to call the numbers, she inevitably made mistakes in their call-names. So when she had the number 31 in her hand she called out "Upstairs and Downstairs", while even a child knows that this is not the name for 31 but for 69. Then the whole game went wrong and she would run out of the room.

She and her husband Levi were not really our Aunt and Uncle, but it was because they lived in the same house as we did for so many years that we considered them as real family. We lived on the third floor and they were down below us. When they came to our building, Duplikate already had six children, and she never missed a chance to beget another one. All together she brought twelve children into this world, or maybe it was fourteen or fifteen. Anyway, the registrar could not keep up with her. Her married life was an endless struggle against lack of money and an endless love-making with Levi. Those two cooed like turtle-doves. Whoever invented the proverb "empty barrels cause quarrels" never had seen Duplikate and her husband billing and cooing.

Levi was a dock worker on a hire-and-fire basis, but he was more fired than hired. Every morning we heard him stumbling through the lower hallway. We could set the clock on him. He walked from Marken Alley where we lived to the docks. With hundreds of other dock workers, all on hire and fire, he stood pushing and wrestling before a huge gate down on the wharf, trying to get in. The bosses on the other side picked from the wriggling ant heap of humans as many dock workers as they figured they could use that day. The "chosen", as those lucky ones were called, were admitted through the gate one after the other in a much-envied single file. The rest of the men remained in the loneliness of the dockside, grumbling, until finally they gave up for that day and stumbled home again.

The bosses chose their dockhands according to their whims, and they had their favourites. The others could starve to death, for all they cared. If a boss had a grudge against you, you could only hope to get work in rush periods when there were more jobs than men on the waterfront. At such times not even a tyrant could leave you outside the gate. But how very seldom periods of over-demand for workers occurred.

Sometimes four or five weeks would pass before there were a couple of steamers in dock which had to be emptied or loaded in a hurry. Then Levi would work first on the day shift, and then again under a false name on the night shift. Sometimes he was very lucky. Under still another false name, he would pick a day shift again, three jobs in a stretch.

When he had done that work for twenty-four hours or longer, sweating under sacks of sugar weighing more than a hundred pounds, and finally knocked off, he would stumble like a cripple back to his house in Marken Alley.

If you added up all the hours, you still could not escape the conclusion that Levi was out of work at least ten months of the year. Now and then he would stand on the cobblestones and try to scratch some money together with a small business of some sort or another. But it was pitiful to see that he did not possess any talent for business. If it is true, as they say, that a businessman is born with a nose for smelling how the market will go, then Levi was born without a nose. By way of speaking, of course, for in reality his face was provided with an imposing schnozzel. When he bought a bunch of skates so cheap that even a blind man could see the profit laying inches thick on the resale, there was sure not be to be a winter that year.

Fortunately, Levi's temperament did not suffer perceptibly under such adversities. He accepted them because he regarded them as being part of life. His face bore an unchanging comical expression, a little bewildered, as if he was surprised each day that he had not yet died of starvation. But it may also be that he was wondering why it was that Duplikate gave birth to child after child. For the numerousness of his offspring, he himself had a rather indistinct explanation. "If I so much as hang my jacket on the bedroom chair, my wife becomes pregnant again," he'd say. But he refused to take his troubles seriously and possessed a stubborn confidence in a happy ending. His philosophy was that if one would live to become 150 years old, everything would turn out all right in the end.

Although there was no hole in the floor through which we could see into the tenement below us, all of us knew that Levi and Duplikate were short of money. It was not considered proper manners to show curiosity about the material situation of neighbours, but we could not disregard it altogether.

So when in our kitchen the pot of lentil soup stood bubbling on the paraffin heater with smoked wurst simmering in it, and the penetrating odour of fried onions and matzoh balls floated through the whole building, Mother would sometimes say "I wonder when was the last time they ate soup down below?"

She asked the question even though she knew the answer, for if Duplikate ever had anything to cook, we would know it from the smell.

"I think I would be doing them down there a big mitzvah if I let them have some of our food," Mother would add.

But how could she do this without giving them the impression that we were intruding? It was an impossible situation. Just one floor below us they had a nest full of children so hungry that their rumbling stomachs could have formed a church choir, while we had plenty to eat. Although money did not grow on my father's back, we did not know real poverty or actual hunger, at least not during the years I am telling of now.

"My food has no taste for me," Mother would say when we were sitting at our table. "We are eating here while those poor sheep downstairs are suffering from hunger only because their parents are too proud to accept help from us."

One of those poor sheep downstairs was Sol, a boy of about my age. He and I were friends, and I ran in and out of Duplikate's flat as if I lived there. Sol felt perfectly at home with us too. Mother had tried a couple of time to learn from him what happened on the floor below, but Sol would not let himself be pumped. Then one morning when Mother unexpectedly entered the kitchen she caught Sol in the act of taking a piece of bread out of the bread basket and trying to hide it under his jacket. I think he and I were about ten years old at the time.

Mother's was startled. "Solomon…what are you doing?" she shouted. But at once she took the poor boy by the hand, hugged him and constraining herself said quietly, "If you want a piece of bread here, you don't need to take it yourself. I'm here to see that everyone gets his share. Give me that roll, then I'll cut it into slices and smear a lick of butter on it. Wait a minute, I'll put some chocolate spread on it for you as well. And I'll get you a glass of milk. Well, enjoy your food!"

Sol began to cram his food down as if he had been on the very brink of starvation. When he had had enough, Mother sent him down in the street to play.

That evening when we were having supper, she told us what had happened afterwards.

"I went downstairs and I told Duplikate 'Listen, maybe it's none of my business, but are you so poor that your children have to steal bread from the neighbours?'"

Now this Duplikate with a belly like a balloon, because there's one on the way again, told me something that if you had read it in the papers you wouldn't believe it. They are broke, absolutely and completely stone broke. There is nothing left in their house that the pawnbroker will find worth looking at, either. You know what that schlemiel, that Levi, told his children last night? 'Those of you who go to sleep without food and do not cry will get a cent for reward.' Can you beat that? Those little kids went to bed without food and without crying, and their father gave each of them one cent, the last few cents he had. But this morning he said 'If you give me back that cent of last night, I will buy bread with it, and then we can all eat.'"

Said Grandma "That Levi should have his head knocked against the wall, that is no mensch, that is a monster. And the same applies to his stupid wife."

But she added immediately, "I hope you told her to send the children to us."

From that day on, it was a matter of course that the neighbours of the first floor ate from our kitchen whenever they wanted. When the large pan with soup for our two families stood on the gas, Grandma sometimes grumbled "Look at the size of that pan, we should rent a hangar for it." Or she would say mockingly to Mother "You'd better call the doctor. We've got parasites."

In the months and years that followed, I believe Sol ate more in our home than at his mother's. He was ridden by an insatiable hunger. Just like his mother, there had not been much brain bestowed on him, but his unending desire for food, and more food, had developed in his character a sort of animal cunning. As far as I know, he did not suffer from any physical handicap but his movements were jerky, he walked with little shocks. There was no grace about him. You got the impression that somewhere deep down in his body there were wires that connected his limbs with his head, and that those wires were twisted and tangled. His muscles seemed to be permanently cramped and he always seemed to have to break a certain tension before he could function. In his frog-like eyes there was a challenging look, an expression of "I take".

At that time, the diamond industry had some prosperity and paid good wages, so my parents decided that it was no longer necessary for us to live in the narrow Marken Alley. They looked around and one day we were able to rent a better situated tenement nearby in Rapenburg Street. This was a considerable improvement, because the back windows offered a view of gardens and a canal. And so we parted from our neighbours.

Aunt Duplikate had red eyes when we packed our bags. She told Mother that she would never forget what she had done for her family. We wished her and Uncle Levi mazzel and broches in his business.

Afterwards we maintained our friendly relations with their family, but naturally the mutual visits became more infrequent. Sol very seldom came to sit at our table any more, after we moved. Now and then we heard news from Duplikate, usually it said that her family had increased again.

We only heard again about Sol when he left school and got a job at the Weesperpoort Railway Station. Wearing a white jacket and carrying a large serving plate, he ran along the trains shouting, "Rolls…nice rolls with salt brisket, wurst, roast beef, cheese! Nice rolls to take along!" His set weekly wage consisted of the capital amount of half a guilder, but he could keep the tips and sometimes these amounted to a full guilder in a week. He told us that ten cents pocket money was enough for him and that the rest of what he earned he gave to his mother. For the first time in her married life, Duplikate had a steady income.

Sol ate at the refreshment bar of the Railway Station and did not have to pay for his food. He ate very well, making it a point to sit down with the manager in the waiting room of the station. Nobody knows how many rolls with salt brisket, wurst, roast beef, and cheese he swallowed every day but it must have been a Himalaya of bread. The steady work and the food appeared to agree with him because he became more balanced, inwardly. Gradually the ravenous look disappeared from his bulging eyes. However, despite all his eating he remained as thin as a locust.

Mother remarked "How that Sol has changed. You really wouldn't recognise him. That work suits him."

I believe that he had been selling rolls along the station platform for a couple of years when the incident with Mr. Sheep occurred.

Mr. Sheep was a small-time jeweler. During a short boom he had earned quite a lot of money and had been brainy enough to make conservative but profitable investments. His wife, Mrs. Sheep was a friend of my mother. One day Mother came back from a visit to the Sheep family and told us that Sol had addressed Mr. Sheep at the station. Although he did not know him at all, he had heard talk about him in our home. "Aren't you Mr. Sheep?" he had asked.

"Yes," Mr. Sheep had replied. "And who might you be?"

That gave Sol his opening, and he told a long story about how he knew Mr. Sheep by name although they had never met. Finally he asked, could he have a private talk with Mr. Sheep? He had a business proposition to put to him.

"Come to my house tomorrow evening," Mr. Sheep had agreed.

That evening Sol went, freshly washed and nervous. He had an idea, he said, to start a shop. In the couple of years at the station he had looked around and heard a few things. To obtain a licence for a buffet at the station was very difficult and he had another idea, a much grander one. He wanted to start a shop in Weesper Street, a small shop with practically no overhead expenses. He would sell rolls and beef of first-rate quality. But that was not all, in the diamond factories there were messenger boys and apprentices who were sent out to buy bread rolls and cakes for the polishers. They bought them in different places but he, Sol, had an idea for monopolising that trade. How? Dead simple, he would be content with a smaller profit and would give the messenger boys a percentage of what they bought from him as a kickback.

The only problem was that he did not have the money to start with, so could Mr. Sheep provide him with a loan of say a thousand guilders. Actually, a loan was not the proper word, Mr. Sheep would get an interest in the business.

"No," Mr. Sheep said firmly. "I wouldn't think of it. I am not a millionaire, and the few guilders that I have are tied in bonds and houses which I cannot sell. I'm sorry, my boy, but you won't get a cent out of me."

The whole affair would have come to nothing if Mrs. Sheep had not been present at this conversation. When her husband announced so curtly that he would not sink a cent in that roll and brisket shop, she said "Listen, what you do with your money is your affair. But I myself have a little nest egg, not much, but just enough to invest in something worthwhile. So I think I'll buy an interest in Sol's undertaking."

When Mr. Sheep started protesting, she announced that she was not his slave.

Time did not stand still but moved, and a new era was coming in which women spoke for themselves. If she had saved a few guilders each week from the household money without her husband noticing, then she was free to spend it anyway she chose.

The exciting story that Mother told us was that her friend, Mrs. Sheep, against her husband's wish, had become a business partner of Sol. Mother gasped indignantly, "I can't imagine a more stupid thing to do. That boy has as much business know-how as his father, so she can say goodbye to her money."

But she was wrong, because soon enough it became apparent that in fact, Sol possessed more business sense in his little finger than old man Levi had in his entire body. He stayed at the Weesperpoort station for another three months and used that time to tell travellers that he was going to start his own business. And could he get their trade, please?

The little shop in Weesper Street quickly became a flourishing affair. Duplikate now came to our home in Rapenburg Street at least once a week, ostensibly to drink a cup of coffee but actually to brag about her son Sol's success. "Such a boy, and chochme he has! Honestly, I don't know where he got it from. Not from me, I'm sure."

"Not from Levi either," Grandma commented.

Duplikate was so full of motherly pride that she did not even notice Grandma's remark, she just continued the-sentence she had started. "Every week he brings money for my household. I bought some linoleum for the floor and some furniture. You must come next week, then you can see it for yourself."

"Sol must be content now, having his own business," said Mother.

Duplikate looked at her with those dumb eyes of hers and replied slowly, "Content? Sol content in his shop? He was only content those first weeks when he ran along the trains in his white jacket. But now he is already saying that he wants to move out of the shop in Weesper Street as soon as he can."

"Well, what does he want then?" asked Mother.

"He has told me, but I don't understand what he means," Duplikate said humbly.

Her son's intentions were however not so inscrutable. One evening when he came to call, he told us quite candidly what he thought about his shop and what he intended to do. "A shop is a good thing to start with, but if you want to be really rich you must not stay in a shop."

"Why not be content with what you have. Thousands of people are jealous of what you earn. Why should you want to become rich?"

"Because I don't want to be poor. I know what poverty is, I know it better than anybody in the world. I want money, and plenty of it. Heaps of it!"

Sol was caught by the power of his own imagination. As if he saw in a vision a mountain of solid gold coins. "Money, so much money that I, that I will…that I will never have to steal bread again. There, now you know why I want it."

A couple of years before the disaster of the German invasion swept over Holland, Sol came to see us. He had come to say farewell. By that time he had sold his shop and had gone into trading things, a dizzying, climbing spiral from one business to another.

Although he was rich, he remained thin and his movements were jerkier than ever. His eyes seemed to estimate everyone and everything, as if he was forever laying in wait and thinking, "What is that man worth? For how much can I buy him?"

He told us he was going to America.

"Why?" Father asked. "You make money enough here."

"I have to go, I have to leave this country. You can call it presentiment. It's just as if something is calling me. I have made financial provisions for my parents and my brothers and sisters. They will not starve, and in case of an emergency I can always send them more money. But for me, I am leaving."

He went to America. Now and then Duplikate came to read a letter to us that she had received from him. He lived in New York, but he did not think he would stay there very long.

After the war, in 1948 the newspaper for which I worked sent me to South America.

I was sitting in the lobby of the Hotel Ambassador in Caracas, when a lively fellow asked me in German if he could offer me a drink.

"*Jawohl*, are you a German?" I asked.

No, he said, he was from Czechoslovakia. Was I German?

"No, I am Dutch," I replied. He had thought that and we talked for a while. Before I left, I had promised him that I would pay him a visit the next day.

In the garden of his house was the fragrant smell of the exotic flowers of Venezuela. But inside the house it was Berlin in the year 1928. Lots of small portraits on the wall, plates with Lebkuchen and Käsekuche on the table. In a corner of the room a couple of guests were sitting at a table playing Skat.

We talked about the olden days when the gay life moved around Kurfuestendamm, and the German Jews still believed in the pipe-dream that they had become Jewish Germans.

Then one of them said, "Aber hier in Caracas wohnt doch…" and he mentioned a rather Spanish sounding name. "Das ist doch ein Holländer. That Hollander vill like to meet you, I think."

And he phoned, half in Spanish, half in German. "Der Herr kommt… The gentleman is coming."

When the visitor entered I recognised him immediately. Sol!

Thin as a wire, still. Restless as ever. Jerky and moving in spurts. Looking around, estimating everything.

We embraced and then shook hands. It had been so many years since we had last met. That evening we talked about old friends and acquaintances. About his father and mother and brothers and sisters. All gone. Gas chambers, all of them.

He invited me to his place next day. He would send a car to the Ambassador. Sol's estate was about an hour's drive from town.

"Estate?"

"Yes, estate."

An estate it was, with farmers who worked for him. With a castle for a house. Garages and four shiny big limousines. Riding horses.

"Are you married, Sol?"

"Sure. She's a beauty, half British, half Spanish. Costs me a fortune each year, that woman. And I have one child. A son. One is enough for me."

"What's his name?"

"We call him Junior."

The car that he sent for me was a Cadillac, and if someone had told me that the accessories were made of pure gold, I would have believed it without hesitation.

The chauffeur was in uniform, a half-caste with the obsequiousness of a slave and the adroitness of a London headwaiter.

It was true, Sol's wife was a glamorous beauty, slender and with gracious movements. His son was a fat little brat about four years old, spoiled and troublesome. I thought he resembled Duplikate a bit, but of course I did not say that aloud.

During the meal, a deluge of food and drinks, a room with noiseless servants, Sol told me that he was still in business. Only now it was big business, very big. In Venezuela he had made loads of money. He had built hotels and sold them again. He had traded in mining claims, had speculated wildly with shady shipping companies along the coast, had traded in pearl fisheries at Santa Madelena. Frankly, he possessed more money than he could count. But he was not content. He wanted more, always more.

After the meal, he and his wife showed me Junior's wing of the house. The four-year-old terror had his own apartment, his own servants who ran after him constantly. In one room, the floor was covered by a huge electric toy railway. Trains with lights, signals that jumped to "Safe" automatically when the tiny carriages had passed. Level crossings that moved mysteriously.

Junior muttered something half in Spanish, half in English. I couldn't understand what he was saying but the child had such an unpleasant, insistent tone in his voice that I thought a spanking would do him good.

"No," Sol said to him, as if he were refusing something. The child kept on whining.

"What does he want?" I asked curiously.

"Oh…, nothing special," said Sol with an awkward glance at me.

His wife explained. "He's saying 'Play Dutchman'. Come on, do it Sol."

"No," said Sol. He was obviously irritated, and he looked about wildly as if he felt driven into a tight corner."

"Play Dutchman," whined the child.

"Let him have his way," I said. The whining irritated me.

"I don't understand why you refuse," said Sol's wife. "Other times you are willing enough."

"Oh, all right then," Sol said grudgingly. Reluctantly he took a silver serving platter from a table, balanced it in his right hand, stood astride the rails of the toy train.

And suddenly, a high-pitched boyish voice rang in the room. Sol shouted, "Nice rolls, nice rolls with salt brisket, wurst, roast beef or cheese…Nice rolls to take on your trip!"

The spoiled little fat son screamed with pleasure. The woman laughed. Sol blushed, as if in shame. For a short second I thought the restlessness had disappeared from his eyes. I don't know why, but suddenly I felt a sort of lump in my throat.

"You remember, Sol," I said hoarsely, "how you used to come to our house to have dinner with us. I remember it as if it were yesterday."

But he cut it off roughly, saying, "Yesterday never returns."

GLOSSARY

Bar Mitzvah   Ceremony held in the synagogue in which the 13-year old Jewish boy reaches the status of a man.

Behayme   Animal.

Behomoth   Cattle. Plural form of behayme.

Ben   Son (of).

Beschrie   Let evil befall on.

Bezel   Cutting side of a diamond.

Broches   Blessings.

Cabala   Occult movement in Judaism.

Carré   Opera house in Amsterdam alongside the river Amstel.

Chachma   Shrewdness.

Culet   Cutting side of diamond.

Chazzer   Pig.

Chanukah The Feast of Light commemorating the victory of the Jewish Maccabees over Syrian despots in 167 B.C. .

Chevrabook Community book.

Girdle Clasp to hold the rough diamond.

Golem Robot. According to Jewish legend the Golem was an artificial human being made of clay and mud.

Gonifed Stolen. From the Hebrew term "gonif" (thief).

Kaddish Prayer at the grave by the children of the deceased.

Kol Voice.

Kol Nidre The plaintive prayer that ushers in Yom Kippur, the Day of Attonement.

Matzoth Plural of "matzoh". Unleavened bread.

Mazel Luck.

Mazel tov Congratulations.

Mazuma Money.

Meiwe Expert.

Meshugge Crazy. A crazy man is a meshuggener, a crazy woman is a meshuggeneh.

Mishpocheh Family.

Narrish Crazy. Idiot.

Nebbish   Term of compassion ("poor man").

Niegish   Superstitious belief that a certain act will bring evil upon that person.

Oy weh   Cry of lamentation.

Pavilion   Side of a diamond.

Pesach   Jewish Passover.

Pièce de Milieu   Table decoration (French).

Rachmones   Compaasion.

Shabbes   Slang for Sabbath, the holy day of the week.

Shlemiel   Simple and unlucky person.

Shmooz   Tale told to escape responsibility.

Simchath   Joy.

Shul   Synagogue.

Tochis   Posterior, behind.

Tsuris   Sorrow.

Unbeschrien–unberufen   Magic saying to fend off evil spirits.

Vodde   Slang for "vodden" (Dutch: "rags").

Wohnt   Lives (German).

Yidd'l mit de Fidd'l   Jew with the fiddle (Yiddish).